Also by Alice Wickenden

POETRY:

To Fall Fable (Variant Lit, 2021)

THRIFTWOOD

Wickenden

for Tony Jay and the 26th Colchester Sea Scouts

ISBN: 978-1-913642-78-5

Cover design by Aaron Kent

Edited & Typeset by Aaron Kent

Broken Sleep Books (2021)

Broken Sleep Books Ltd
Rhydwen,
Talgarreg,
SA44 4HB
Wales

Contents

Camp Three: The 22nd World Scout Jamboree, Sweden

Interlude: 1 May 2012

Thriftwood:
A Personal History of Scouting

Alice Wickenden

Introduction.

Those old melodies still sound so good to me / As they melt the years away (The Carpenters, 'Yesterday Once More')

i

I haven't slept in a tent in years. Perhaps this isn't that unusual? I'm in my mid-twenties. At this age, once you've grown out of family camping holidays (assuming both that yours was the sort of family who could afford such holidays and that you were raised by the sorts of people who took pleasure in such trips) when would you? Very few of my friends still camp, although the number is slowly trickling back up as we settle down into our own adulthoods, measure out the sticky ghost shapes left by our parents, look for something affordable to do. Find ourselves gasping for fresh air. Then there are festivals, of course, although I'm not sure they count, those drunken, stoned, sticky nights, when the tent acts as mere reprieve rather than the reason for you to be there in the first place. No festival tent is ever *home*.

And anyway, I haven't camped at a festival since 2014. I don't drink much anymore, if at all – especially not spirits – but the last real memory I have of life in a tent is of sitting cross-legged, doing bright and too-sweet shots of bootleg melon liquor bought in some anonymous duty free, eating the remnants of a giant lemon cake for breakfast, washing the stale crumbs down with cider and gin. Everything that weekend was alcohol-tinged and filthy, and Chris and I, who had once been in love with the same girl – although he didn't know, yet, that when she'd left him briefly it had been for me – were getting grimly drunk enough to face the trek back to the train station and then the journey back to London. Those return journeys are memorable mostly for the way we moved from being part of a tattooed and buoyant crowd to wastrels, outsiders: the crowd slowly ebbing out, a collective dispersal.

We drank even more on the final train back but now that we were no longer festival-goers it just felt sordid. Suddenly, we were just two slightly pissed almost-20-year-olds who hadn't washed for days, smelling of smoke and sweat and music. The commuting adults – who might in their past have been us – decisively avoided eye-contact, afraid of whatever we represented. That final trip back, we had left our cheap, broken tent there: a decision I still feel guilty about in terms of the environment and the way it so accurately captures that careless relationship to cheap plastic dispossession that I am only now unlearning, which also seems symbolically poignant. It was, after all, an ending (several endings, as it turned out) as much as an abandonment.

Although my parents did take me and my siblings camping as children, the real reason that I ever camped enough to miss its absence as viscerally as I do now is that I was a Scout. I say that like it's a confession. But it means *something*. Not many people guess, if they didn't know me from eleven to eighteen, and when I tell them they always seem to forget it, are surprised all over again when it comes up: when my muscle memory kicks in and I tie a perfect reef knot, or when I casually talk about having gutted fish. I know why. I live in London now and have never been successful at either exercising or leaving the city; I no longer hike, except for family holidays with relatives who live in the countryside and own dogs and chickens; I read too much, am accumulating literature degrees like clutter. I don't have a garden, of course, having traded outdoor space for the dubious acclamation of a vaguely central city location, and no amount of houseplants can make the urban lifestyle resemble that of someone properly 'outdoorsy'. And then, finally, no matter how close the relationship between literature and the outside world, it still seems to confuse some people that you might cross between the two, or that you might want to – that *I* might want to. God, how I want to.

Anyway, I get cold really easily, and I like the middle-class trappings of my mid-twenties life: cooking with parmesan, going to the theatre, woollen blankets and second-hand cashmere jumpers, too-expensive coffee that's been lingered over. None of these attributes scream Scout. I'm aware of that.

My first ex-boyfriend James, on the other hand, has stayed in Scouts. His dad was a troop leader, and I still remember with an unsettled awe the way his older brother would come back in the university holidays (where he played Ultimate Frisbee, a fact that sums up that family more than anything else could) and immediately throw himself into helping run the Troop. It was in their blood, or perhaps their bones: a sinew-deep connection to the outside. James was never going to leave Scouts – and he hasn't. He still climbs, runs, and wears fleeces: he still does Jailbreak, a 24-hour event where groups of Scouts on foot try to evade their leaders who are on bikes. Except now he's on the other side: he's a climbing instructor, a good and patient man who runs extreme races with his girlfriend – for *fun* – and encourages children to face their fears. When I spoke to him about this project, he told me an anecdote about how he'd helped a girl get to the top of the climbing wall who at the beginning of the session had been too scared to try. At the closing meeting she had said it was her favourite part of the camp, and he had cried with pride. Telling me the story over a poor internet connection, we both welled up; Scouting can be so good, so important, it can do so much. But he was always much more tangibly, obviously part of that world.

I remember, at sixteen, asking him to wear jeans to a party instead of his normal combat trousers. I was embarrassed at the prospect of an obvious intrusion of the coarser life of Scouts into the social one I was constructing alongside it. And I was embarrassed at my own embarrassment. I was just as terrified he'd challenge me – that he'd ask why I was dating him in the first place, if I didn't like his trousers – as I was that he'd forget my request and wear them anyway. He didn't; he wore jeans. The power imbalance in that relationship was tilted in my favour, or at least it was when we were in my domain, my town. Sure, he was a year older – point to him – but I was conventionally pretty; he was nerdier, although I was cleverer; most importantly, probably, he liked me far more than I liked him, and we both knew it.

By now, you might be thinking that I was not a nice person at sixteen, and it might be true.

In that other world, where James and I had met in the first place, he had the edge. He was better with his hands. He was stronger and knew more than me about how to build things, how to be practical, how to *survive*. (This seems like an exaggeration, and I'm always reminded of that *Peep Show* episode where Mark and Jeremy get lost in the Cotswolds: 'Nobody is gonna die, this is Southern England. Nobody dies in Southern England, Jeremy, that just doesn't happen' – but the point is, even if we were never in any real danger, it felt like we could be. Surely one of the main attractions of camping is the way it feels tangential to risk?) One of my favourite memories of the two of us is of a night on camp where a majority of our Unit – 15 of us, at least – decided to sleep outside. We dragged our sleeping bags and ground mats out once the leaders had gone to sleep (or pretended to) and put them around the embers of the fire. The stars were bright. At least, they are in my imagination, but there is no reason why they couldn't have been in real life too; it must have been reasonably warm, clear enough that we could be confident of avoiding rain. Normally, girls and boys aren't allowed in each other's tents – a rule which was to become one of the defining ones of my relationship to Scouting – but suddenly that boundary had disappeared.

James and I usually occupied an uneasily subdued relationship around other people, uncomfortable with displaying any signs of sexuality, or even a particular enjoyment of the other's company. That sort of vulnerability demands a security we didn't have as teenagers, or in our own emotions. That might be unfair on him, actually: I'm sure *he* had that security, that he was acting according to a distance I imposed. I'm sure I was the one who kept him at arm's length when others were around. But not that night, when we drew our sleeping bags up next to each and slept close together. Somehow, being cocooned alongside him was more intimate than being in the same bed. More intimate again because my friend Caz was pressed close to my other side, whilst he was bookended by someone else. (It might have been Morgan – devastatingly attractive, with cheekbones and an obsession with cars, who would go on to DJ in Cambridge and run into me every so often, a reminder that I couldn't quite leave Scouts behind – or Kyle, simultaneously sincere and wry.) We slept like that, pressed together like puppies, under the sky.

At least we slept that way until about 3am when a fox jumped straight into the middle of the huddle. Even now I can't think what it was after. Foxes are rife on sites, and more than one of my friends had at some point had a piece of clothing stolen (there was a particular fox in Thorrington, Essex, with a real fondness for men's trainers and an uncanny ability to sense the weak parts of tents, a renowned menace) but that leap into a huddled pack of teenagers went against everything I knew about the animal. Maybe it was cold enough to risk it, searching for mammalian heat. Or maybe it knew something sacred was happening: a communion of some sort, a promise. Either way, it woke us all up; someone screamed and the spell broke; the cold snapped at us; the leaders couldn't pretend not to know what was going on and had to come out to tell us to get back inside our damn tents *now*. We were all faintly relieved, I think, to avoid the inevitable disappointment of the next morning, when the night had stopped glimmering. James and I peeled apart and went our separate, abashed ways until breakfast, when everyone collectively re-gathered in the mess tent and regaled all those who hadn't joined us with the tale of our night spent under the stars. Basking in the glorious, tepid friction of being slightly in trouble.

The real reason I find it so odd that people no longer associate me with Scouting is that it was *everything* to me. For years it was the heart of my social life, my emotional life, and – yes – overwhelmingly my sexual life as well, stuttering and awkward as that was. It nurtured nestled threads of trauma and friendship that would come to define teenagehood and puberty for me, and that still entangle me now. Scouts is a story I have never told but am always living. People think they know what it means, but they do not, cannot, not unless they lived it too. I have never left it behind.

ii.i

MAYBE we should start with some facts and definitions. (These apply to UK Scouting only.)

- *Colony*: Beaver Scouts, 6-8 years old.
- *Pack*: Cub Scouts, 9-11 years old.
- *Troop*: The fundamental unit of a Scout group. Members are aged (roughly) 11-14 years old.
- *Unit*: The name for a group of Explorer Scouts, 15-18.

Beavers, Cubs, and Scouts, work at a whole-group level. That is to say, you are inducted into each section separately, but they fall under the same Troop 'banner'. My Troop both *was* and was *part of* the 26th Colchester Sea Scouts: I joined when I left Brownies at 11, meaning that I skipped both Beavers and Cubs and came in straight as a Scout.

By most external metrices, we were not the best group in Colchester. Certainly we were poorer and less well attended than our rival Troop, the 17th, who did 'proper' activities like sailing. Both our Troops had boat huts on Mersea, which is a mudflat-ridden island in Essex about half an hour's drive from Colchester. It's connected to the mainland by the Strood – a causeway which gets flooded at high tide, leaving you stranded – so there was always the sense that going there for an evening was a bit of a gamble. Could you trust the term's programme to have been made with the tides in mind? Either way, the 17th's hut was gleaming and polished whilst ours was – to put it mildly – a bit of a shithole; we spent many evenings of backbreaking work cleaning it, painting it, fixing it up, and seemingly making very little process. We never once sailed – gossip went that Tony, our leader, didn't like the water, a fact my Dad still finds hilarious – but our official 'Sea Scout' designation meant that we had a uniform which consisted of eminently superior blue shirts instead of brown, and neckers which were dark navy hemmed with a lighter blue and decorated with an anchor motif. When I joined Jenny, Tony's wife, sewed them by hand. Towards the end of my time in the 26th she had to stop due to arthritis and our anchor design became a badge instead, at which point having a hand sewn necker became a mark of a certain authority.

Unless we were doing something which required clothes you could get dirty in, shirts were required for the weekly meetings. Full uniform – which meant ironed shirts, badges up to date, carefully rolled (and ideally also clean) neckers with the right amount of folds, smart black or navy trousers and sensible black shoes – were only needed for public events, like the carol service or St George's Day Parade. On camp, though, the only uniform requirement would be to have the necker on at all times: taking it off was considered an incursion of the rules. After a whole week, it would be sweat-stained where your skin had been in constant contact, reeking of fire and usually lake-water too. The light blue hem tinged with mud and smoke. Most nights on camp I would sleep in it, too – partly for warmth, but partly because it seemed wrong to take it off – and at home once it had been washed, I kept it tied to the headboard of my bed.

In contrast to the Colony, Pack, and Troop, Explorer Units are technically organised on a District wide level. However, it's common in practice for a Unit to be set up in association with a pre-existing Troop. Our Unit was called *Endeavour*, and although it was technically open to anyone, it was mostly treated like a continuation of the 26th, something which treated us just fine. This was especially true since our Unit leader, CJ, was Tony's son. There were two pre-existing Units in Colchester – called *Tsunami* and *Destiny*, they always sounded like colonial ships – but their associations with the 17th rendered them unacceptable to our little scrabble of friends. They were looming, unfriendly, and full of people we didn't know with skills we might not be able to match. We needed a place of our own. As a result, *Endeavour* was set up the year I turned fifteen.

Since 1991 UK Scout groups have accepted both boys and girls, although this was optional until 2000. This means that the UK Girl Guiding association runs parallel to the Scouting movement, although it still only accepts girls; gender divisions remain more entrenched in the US, hence references to 'Girl Scouts' and 'Boy Scouts'. The divisions here work more or less the same, but apart from Brownies – who are in a 'Pack' – the groups are all known as Units.

- *Rainbows*, 5-7 years old.
- *Brownies*, 7-10 years old.
- *Guides*: 11-14.
- *Rangers*: 15-18.

Both Girl Guides and Boy Scouts were founded by Robert Baden-Powell. It was more or less designed as training for the British Army. Does this matter, its inherent colonialism, its racism, its intended purpose to serve the Empire? Does it change anything?

ii.ii

WHEN you become a Scout, you take a Promise. The whole Troop watches you. You salute the flag, make the Scout sign with your left hand, and say:

> "On my honour I promise that I will do my best
> to do my duty to God and to The Queen,
> to help other people
> and to keep the Scout Law."

Other, non-Christian variants are available, although I'm not sure I ever heard anyone use them. The Christianity of Scouts is both superficial and intrinsic, in ways few eleven-year-old children would notice. I have never believed in God – or in the Queen, for that matter – but I remember how I felt the impact of every word land heavy on me. It all seems so *nationalist* now, raising and lowering the flag at the beginning of every meeting (being careful not to let it touch the floor, which I almost invariably, accidentally did, every time I was tasked with this job) but at the time it seemed right, bravely ceremonial. Repeating those words that children had said for years was a way of opening up membership of something that you would belong to for life, like it or not. I remember TJ telling me before I went off to university that throughout my life I would meet people who were Scouts, who wanted to talk to me about it, as if the entire organisation were an old-boy's network, an informal lattice of people stretching across the globe. I liked the idea of belonging, always.

The rhythm of the Promise as a piece of verse still seems perfect to me now. The line breaks as I've written it out above mimic the staccato way I memorised it, the same way we remember mobile phone numbers in patterns: at eleven, it seemed impossible to treat as a whole. *On my honour I promise...* honour is such a strange thing to demand of a child, such a weighty word, but then it's instantly undone: all you have to promise is to *do my best*. Anyone can do that. It's a great piece of writing. The zeugma of 'to' – I will do my best *to* do my duty *to* God and *to* the Queen – see how easily those different uses of 'to' fall into a pattern, a poem, an incantation, until you are promising something of yourself, giving yourself to the future? And once you shake the leader's hand, that's it: you're a Scout now. You can rejoin the ranks as one of them. And slowly, over the years, you watch people go through the same ritual, and you learn to repeat it to yourself, mutter it along with them, and every time a promise is made new.

ii.iii

IT seems strange that it was only upon thinking through these associations with the flag that I remembered that our Scout hut when I joined was actually in the old Army barracks. Without any sense of the politics involved, I grew up adjacent to the military: Colchester is a garrison town. In practice, this means that the Army seeps into the daily fabric of life long before you have the ability to unpick it: it shapes your relationships, your town, your education. Several classmates at school and friends in Scouts had parents in the military. My Year 6 teacher was married to a soldier. My parents' house was near the garrison and it was not uncommon for impressively fit groups of men in camouflage to run by the windows or to pass us as we were walking into town. For a few weeks in school I did some work experience in one of the Primary schools attached to the Garrison and talked to children who moved every year, or more. We learnt to swim in the Army pool, and at seventeen, the field next to the barracks was where I would go to kiss people secretly. If you grow up in a space like that, it moulds you, pushing back so that you can only ever trace out your own memories and associations within it. Ours was a town that always had a military presence, but as a fairly blithe and unobservant child it was rarely explicit for me other than at the moments that the rhythms of Army life broke through: the sounding of gun salutes, helicopters buzzing their insect drone overhead, the muffled intrusions of a world of violence. How could I be unbiased? How can anyone? I distrust the Army, politically, ideologically, morally, but I have loved people in it.

When our Troop was there, the old barrack buildings were mostly empty: huge Victorian red-bricks that have now mostly been demolished for one of the more soulless housing blocks I've ever come across. There were some horses pastured there. I remember one evening wandering off to look at them with a new girl at scouts, a girl I had a brief, passionate, pre-teen obsession for before she left, the sort of friendship you look back on a decade later and think *ohhhh*. We looked at them rather than at each other and she told me about horse riding. She lives in France now – we have each other on Facebook. I have often wondered about asking her if she remembers that night but then I think, why would she?

I don't know. Maybe she would. You can never predict what will stick. This book that you're reading now – it's just what stuck for me. As I wrote, I sent bits to various friends mentioned, and their memories were completely different. Not in content necessarily, although always also that, but in tone. The most glorious summer of your life, it turns out, can be totally indifferent for someone else. Even when it was them and their presence which helped make it so wonderful. Or they say – oh *yes*, that year – didn't you go off with that boy – as if that decision didn't shatter my life – but then, well, why should they think otherwise? I'm not so solipsistic as to think that they should remember the past through my actions, or at least I'd like not to be, even though I probably am. Anyway. These are my memories. Most of them I wrote down in my diaries at the time – diligent teenage scribbling, recording the sincerest angst. Most of them, it turns out, I didn't need to. Or maybe, paradoxically, I remember *because* I wrote them down.

My dream of an alternate world is not one where the events recounted here didn't happen: it is just of one where I didn't remember it like I did, where I didn't let the desire to make sense of the past corrode the future.

We weren't in the Army barracks for long whilst I was there – a year at most. Or maybe it's just that I remember those evenings less because I was younger, less important to the Troop, the Troop less important to me. Primarily I remember the way that it was fucking freezing in that hall, the way that I would wear two pairs of tights under my jeans even if we were staying inside all evening, and the way that sometimes when I got home my Dad would have left a hot water bottle in my bed. I don't remember an awareness of the military connection, though I think there was a rusted sign in the corridor warning us about something once-dangerous, now forgotten. It was a fairly large room with an old piano in one corner – yes, that's right, an orchestra also used it to practice, so there were lots of plastic chairs stacked up and a cupboard full of music stands – and several dinged metal cupboards that didn't lock properly. I had no strong attachment to it, really, but I ventured there alone and timid and I came out a Scout, so maybe it meant something to me after all.

When they were building there, by the way, they found the remains of a Roman Circus, the only one so far discovered in Britain. Colchester was the Roman capital, for a while; that's why Boudicca stormed it. I like the idea of those layers of history. The Roman chariots being replaced by the Army ones, then being replaced again by two girls looking at some grazing horses, fumbling towards something profound to say.

Camp One: Thriftwood, 2006

So I put my hands up / They're playing my song, / And the butterflies fly

away (Miley Cyrus, 'Party in the USA')

iii

SHE*is eleven, and a week feels like eternity. She arrives prompt, loud and showing off in the car on the way to disguise the unmistakable bite of nerves, the coil in her stomach that hissed last night when she tried to sleep. She has a rucksack that seems to weigh almost as much as her that she packed and repacked with an anxious crumpled list for reference, and pinching brand new walking boots she promised she'd wear in and didn't. she has her mum's phone number memorized, and an old sleeping bag that belonged to her dad, and a week stretches out in front of her, almost unbearably long, almost forever.*

And she almost wants to say: please take me back with you. *She is still not 100% sure she wants to be here; already she has almost left once. The night she got invested. New, too-large prickly shirt, brushed hair and carefully chosen jewellery –* you're not going to a party *her mum laughed at her and she took it off when nobody was watching – and after they had made their vows, saluted the flag, shaken their leader's hand, they played a game involving eating dry food with your hands behind your back, as quickly as possible. Scarfing down weetabix, a boy was suddenly, violently sick* on the table in front of her. She remembers the utter horror flooding her body, and the next day having dwelled on it for more than twenty-four hours she told her parents very formally, an admission of failure, I'm not sure I want to be a Scout anymore.

Besides, it's not like she's the type. She isn't really outdoorsy. She's clumsy, and she likes to read, and she isn't very good at making friends, which is maybe why her parents want her to be here in the first place. Everyone else seems loud and brash and she finds them difficult to talk to, and she knows it makes her seem rude and up herself, like she thinks she's too good for them, but she still stays silent rather than say the wrong thing. A few weeks in, they do work for the drama badge: the troop divides up into two groups, and write scripts, which they'll perform the next week. She sits in a corner listening as a gaggle of loud older boys plan their Office rip-off. She is eleven: she has never seen The Office. They cast her as the silent, mousy boss, who doesn't get any of the jokes, until the end scene where she suddenly flips and fires the hero. The joke is that she speaks up. She doesn't care that it's at her expense: she is thrilled and treasures the script for years.

Despite all this uncertainty, then, she is here, ready for a week away for the first time. She went away with Brownies, but it wasn't the same: they had to know where you were, everything was organized and stifled and they slept in sleeping bags inside a hall. Here, they can do anything, roam the woods at will, skive off all the activities and entertain themselves if they want. As long as they're careful. And as long as they look out for one another. The leader is

28

very clear about that.

She has never met anyone like the leader before. It will take her years to understand that she probably never will again.

The plot seems to stretch on forever. She steps out of the car, puts on a brave face, and picks up her bag.

iv

I first went to Thriftwood in 2006, the summer after I joined Scouts. We had a week-long camp every year. A few Cubs and Beavers would join for a couple of days, but for the majority of the time it was just us, usually about 20 kids, 4 or 5 adults. That first time, all I knew about my destination was that Thriftwood was a campsite about an hour's drive away. I knew nothing specific about what to expect. A week is an incredibly long time when you're eleven and even more so when the days seem shapeless, when you can't quite picture what you'll be doing, how you can possibly spend all that time outside. I didn't have a mobile phone, I'd just left Primary school, everything about the future seemed unmoored. The potential for great fun, yes, but also the potential that everything was going to go cripplingly, horribly wrong.

I was bitingly nervous. I had a couple of sort-of friends who were going – Sophie, who was in my class at school, and who I'd joined the 26th with in the first place because her older sister was a Scout there, and Ellie and Sarah, who I also knew from school – but I didn't think of any of them as close friends. Ellie and I had always had a slight enmity because her mum sometimes looked after my best friend, Hannah, after school, a fact that had caused some deep rift between them. It felt personal: none of us could have articulated what it was actually about, which was more to do with class than Hannah's personality. Ellie thought Hannah was stuck-up, which she probably was in the same sort of way I was, and Hannah thought Ellie was whiny. This division had not been helped by an incident earlier that year when Hannah had accidentally hacked our school computer network (with me as a passive onlooker), changing the file names of photos of people in our class. She thought it was just on her account, but it ended up being school wide, and the teachers were, rightly, furious. We got away with it because they liked us: we were clever, and after all, we hadn't *meant* it. I don't even think my parents were told. Ellie was renamed 'stupid', another girl was 'bitch', a boy called Charles 'chicken legs'. (I can't remember now why he'd had that nickname, but unlike the other two, we were close to being friends with him; he was my first experience of flirtation.) This whole thing was, obviously, petty and callously cruel. I don't want to make allowances for my childhood self. Children can be as bigoted and mean as teenagers. We had thought we were getting back at people who were cooler than us and who made us feel awkward, not realising the ways in which it was our own shyness and burgeoning intellectual snobbery that made us aloof and dismissive.

Anyway, although we'd apologised sincerely, I still felt

uncomfortable around Ellie. We'd more or less been enacting an uneasy truce since we found ourselves thrown into the same Troop, but this summer was different. We no longer *had* to be around each other every day. This was that undefined limbo before Proper Secondary Education, meaning not only that soon we'd be in different schools, but also that Scouts would suddenly be the only link left between. I think we were both vividly aware that if things were otherwise there'd have been no link other than the past left at all: we lived on the same road, so we might have seen each other on the street occasionally to nod to, but that would have been it. Instead here we were, suddenly, and before I knew it we were sharing a tent together. For a whole week.

I was used to camping. My family did it regularly: holidays with my parents in one 'pod', me and my sister in another, my brother in with one group or the other and then eventually on his own. Once a year, my dad and his friends would take us 'Dads' camping' – at its peak this was 6 or 7 families. Our mums would stay home and have a weekend to themselves; the dads would buy us fish and chips on the Friday night and have a whiskey and cheese night whilst we entertained ourselves in the woods fighting vicious battles, boys against girls, building dens. (Don't underestimate it as play: the stakes were high. One year, a kid from another group pulled a penknife on a boy named Peter and the intrusion of something that belonged to the world outside the campsite shocked us. It was so *violating*.) Although there was an obvious heterosexual normativity to these weekends that grated on me even at the time (wasn't it unfair, didn't my mum want to go camping? if I ever had my own children, would I be expected to stay home?) I don't think my mum or any of the other women minded as, by all accounts, their free weekends were raucous fun. For my siblings and I, Dads' camping quickly took on a semi-mythical life of its own. The site we went to was part of Thetford Forest, which is a manmade pine-tree forest and incredibly creepy. The area was famous for UFO sightings and if you wandered far enough into the wood there would be 'alien trail' signs. Of course, we loved it.

However, all this experience aside, I had never really done most of the practical parts of camping. I had never put a tent up by myself before, normally half-heartedly helping my parents before sloping off with my sister instead. This was our first task at Thriftwood, and it seemed close to insurmountable. What the *hell* were we doing? We looked around for inspiration.

Everyone older was pitching their tents as if the poles were extensions of themselves, clicking together like ballet. It took the three of us what seemed like hours. We thought it was a good idea to put it under a tree. It wasn't: if you do this, your tent isn't any more protected when it rains. Water carries on dripfalling through the leaves. More importantly, it's actually more dangerous if there's a storm: the tree threatens to fall on you, lightning is more of a risk. Of course, we didn't know any of this until it was finally up, when our leader came over to check in. He told us off and we had to move it. Everyone was pissed off. That was Tony's style: he'd sit back and let you make any mistake you wanted, but in the end you'd only ever make that mistake once.

I only ever hated him for it when it came to Max.

That evening, we were given an unwieldy metal grill and taught how to light a fire.

1. Find some small branches.

2. Collect kindling (you need a penknife for this; silver birch bark works well. Otherwise, any dry wood will do. Whittle it with the knife and collect the shavings).

3. Make a little den, as if the shavings are playing at protection, so that as they light and curl up on themselves in agony, the fire can spread.

4. Feed it, slowly, dry wood increasing in size, working up to big planks. You have to go down to the woodpile to get these. Some are jagged with skintraps: nails, huge splintering pieces. It takes two to carry the planks, and by the end of it you're

out of breath and sore. You'll learn. Some of the older girls can carry multiple planks by themselves, and know how to pick the best ones, the ones the fire will tongue instantly, the ones that burn as if they were born to it. On your first camp you'll find yourself straggling back with cruel misshapen wood, rotten-dust wood, ugly dark-knotted rust-wood.

5. *It all burns the same in the end*, Tony would say, gruffly, and it does.

We learnt how to build the fire up, huge and hungry, and then to let it die down in order to cook on the embers. We nibbled biscuits whilst we worked and chopped vegetables and chicken on rickety tables in the main camp tent. It took hours: none of us were good cooks. We overcooked the noodles and burned the peppers. But it was still unmistakably stirfry, and delicious.

That night, the three of us shivered together in our sleeping bags, giddy with the freedoms and possibilities ahead. The weirdness of the situation hit us like a wave. As if gasping for breath from the newness of this place, suddenly we found ourselves giggling. I remember realising suddenly – stupidly – that I could actually like these girls, that they were not who I had thought, that maybe neither was I.

It had gone midnight, easily. Towards the end of the week we'd go to bed earlier but those first few nights were precious in their length. Whatever time it was, high on sugar, the lack of parental control, on *being at Thriftwood*, we wriggled down and pretended to be sperm in condoms. We were eleven – the logistics of this game were far less important than its sense of being forbidden. What did we know about sex? I remember only snippets from school sex education: a teacher dropping a tampon in a glass of water to demonstrate how it expanded (do not do this – ever – unless you want to be absolutely horrified); listening to and analysing the lyrics of the Beautiful South's 'A Little Time', for reasons that were obscure then and are baffling now; watching a video on puberty starring a family who went about their day inexplicably naked; being divided by our bodies and shown mysterious videos made even more incomprehensible in the metaphors they reached for to be relatable. The three of us lay in our tent, crammed in next to each other, and reached up with our legs to the top of the tent, which had been deemed 'the egg'. We were flailing, falling over, deciding which brands of condoms we each were, being as explicit and as uncertain as we dared. When you're not quite a teenager, talking about sex is its own kind of vulnerability: how much do you know, how do you mimic the language of adulthood, how much ignorance are you willing to let be seen? Sex education has a lot to answer for.

Slowly, the air heated up. In the morning it would be stifling. In a small tent you quickly learn the perils of trying to layer up at night. You warm up quicker with less clothing in the first place, as illogical as that seems, and you dehydrate less as you sleep. For now, though, wrapped in multiple jumpers, spluttering with laughter over the slippery idea of sex, we fell asleep.

It was not that sudden, as if one day we were not friends and the next we were. But it was a start, I'll always think of that night playing condoms with Ellie as the start: of our friendship, of loving Scouts, of loving Thriftwood. In all its childlike ridiculousness that night is the answer when I worry, sometimes, that everything was always tainted with sex.

ONE night in the woods can change everything. Think of the pairs of tricked and confused lovers in Shakespeare's *A Midsummer Night's Dream* – given a happy ending, as long as you don't mind that Demetrius is going to be under the influence of a love potion for the rest of his life. Without resorting to such measures, how can you resolve a spurned-love plotline? Someone would always have to lose.

When the Lord of Athens, Theseus demands an explanation for what's gone on from the four runaways after their fairy-struck night in the woods, Demetrius offers this confused one, explaining that he followed the lovers Lysandre and Hermia in order to thwart their plot and gain Hermia's love for himself, only to find that in doing so he seems to have lost all desire for Hermia and fallen in love with the always-loyal, once-spurned Helena:

Demetrius: My lord, fair Helen told me of their stealth,
Of this their purpose hither to this wood,
And I in fury hither followed them,
Fair Helena in fancy following me.
But, my good lord,I wot not by what power –

> But by some power it is – my love to Hermia,
>
> Melted as the snow, seems to me now
>
> As the remembrance of an idle gaud
>
> Which in my childhood I did dote upon ...

One night in the woods melts away childhood fancies 'as the snow' and replaces them with adult ones, securing the status quo. We see this time and time again in fairy tales and in children's literature. Travelling through the wood is a metaphor for growing up. Red Riding Hood, confronting the dangers of the forest, loses her safety and naïvety – and possibly her family, depending on which version you read – but is rewarded with a man; Snow White flees from the unwanting family into domestic bliss as housekeeper for not one dwarf but seven, and then is rewarded with a man; Rapunzel's salvation comes in escaping the woods she's been held prisoner, for a man. What about young adult books? *Harry Potter and the Deathly Hallows*, the seventh and final in the series, presents a camping journey darkly contrasted to the festival-like atmosphere of the Quidditch World Cup in *Harry Potter and the Goblet of Fire.* Harry, Ron and Hermione have left their respective families behind: they are not camping for sport or pleasure, but fleeing through dark and dangerous woods anonymously. And of course, when adult emotions blossom – Ron's jealousy and lust, Harry's powerless fury,

Hermione's quiet desperation – the woods are as much to blame as anything or anyone else.

More often, I think, wandering into the woods comes at the start of the young adult adventure, where the protagonists get lost or are forced into lostness, forced into puberty and growing up, taking on their heroic costumes. You'll be thinking of something personal to you; for me, it's the start of Chris Riddell's *Beyond the Deepwoods*, book one of the *Edge Chronicles* 'Twig Saga' (first to be written but narratively, chronologically second). Maybe the Forbidden Forest is a more accurate Potter-point of comparison. So, too, is Shakespeare's Forest of Arden, where – superficially, at least – hierarchical statuses can be overcome or at least overlooked.

This is different, though. The wood of *Midsummer* is not one to journey through as much as it is one to get lost in, and eventually end up back where you started – only better. When Lysander is planning their escape, he tells Hermia:

Lysander: I have a widow aunt, a dowager
Of great revenue, and she hath no child.
From Athens is her house remote seven leagues,
And she respects me as her only son.
There, gentle Hermia, may I marry thee,
And to that place the sharp Athenian law
Cannot pursue us. If thou lovest me then

> Steal forth thy father's house tomorrow night,
>
> And in the wood, a league without the town,
>
> Where I did meet thee once with Helena
>
> To do observance to a morn of May,
>
> There will I stay for thee.

The plot is simple: they'll travel through the wood to a place which is importantly not-Athens, to get married. But that last detail might make us pause. The 'morn of May' is May Day, the festival celebrating the coming of spring. Even before we know it is enchanted, the woods are marked as a place of change, of growth, of *becoming what you are supposed to be*. And, ultimately, the important difference between the woods of *A Midsummer Night's Dream* and *The Deathly Hallows* on one hand and of the fairytales on the other is that the characters sleep in it. In some productions of the Shakespeare – I'm thinking especially of the Bridge Theatre's 2019 one, where the forest scenes were populated by ivy-twined bunk-beds – the sleeping scenes are made deliberately domestic. Sleep is important for the plot, of course, since Puck's magical flower must be laid on sleeping eyelids, but it also offers a suggestion: sleeping in the woods, however temporarily, changes you. Whether that's towards adulthood or something else remains to be seen.

vi

THE rhythm of the days stretches and compresses time until it must be shapeless outside the camp, it is sludgy instant hot chocolate-fluid, it fizzes. 2006: they don't have phones, watches make her wrist itch, so they float untethered by minutes or even hours. In the morning one patrol (6-8 Scouts) will cook breakfast. They took the orders the night before. It is thick with grease: fried bread, fried sausages, fried bacon and fried eggs, burnt baked beans, the one pan of veggie sausages standing proud and usually a little raw. White cheap bread to mop up the grease. Another patrol washes up – at home she would be grossed out by the stringy bacon residue and congealed tomato sauce, but here you can't bother with that disgust, so you simply don't – whilst the rest go and stoke up the campfire, warm up, shower, get dressed. Usually there's three scheduled activities in the day. They do go-karting and shove pickaxes into a dirty grey 'ice' polystyrene wall. The climbing boots are spiked and heavy: you have to kick the wall with all your might. Only the older boys are strong enough to do it properly, the rest spend the majority of the hour hanging there limply, and her arms strain unused to this sort of movement, and the harness threatens pain. And yet: everything about it seems to sparkle. Up there with Sarah shouting lighthearted jokes from below (a few meters at best) she thinks suddenly about the word accomplishment. *This nebulamoment right here might be what people mean.*

There are three boys on the camp they know more-or-less well. One day they burn fiberglass on the fire. The tree above shrinks in repulsion. Its leaves curl up and quickly die brown. Everyone coughs dramatically and wonders loudly about poisoning; at least one girl cries. Holly's mum has gone home by this point, or she would be complaining, not because she is particularly neurotic but because adults mind more about these things. For half an hour the camp is black with noxious air. The leader rolls his eyes and makes the boys do extra cleaning duties. The next day, Ellie comes out of the tent and catches them throwing a bottle of literal shit onto the fire 'for fun'. They discuss this in hushed voices that night: why? Why do boys do these things? It would just never occur to any of them to shit in a bottle and put it on a fire, and certainly not a fire other people have access to. They do one of piss, too, and it explodes, raining the boys in their own hot urine as the girls shriek in dismay. It is a sound of disgust, a protest, an interrogation. Why are you bringing this, the body, into this space? Don't you understand what that might do? Don't you understand that it is dangerous? Don't you understand what we could lose?

Plus, for a few hours, the camp reeks of piss.

44

vii.i

BY the end of that first week in Thriftwood, there were four of us, and we settled into the roles of friendship. I was quiet, sarcastic, slightly reserved. Ellie was tall, blonde, and she talked more freely about her adoption and her family than I'd ever imagined anyone would: she was generous with her intimacies, kinder than I'd suspected, and bitingly funny. Sarah, small and wry and owlish, had long been her best friend, and offered a pleasing balance in both personality and looks.

Ellie picked up the ways of our new half-wild life quicker than anyone else. She gained a reputation for fire-enchanting, everyone calling her over to have a go with their damp, sad kindling: half joking, half reverent. Holly completed us: Holly, who didn't stay in our tent because her mum came with her for a few days, meaning we didn't get to know her straight away. She had joined the Troop fairly recently. She had a weird knitted purple bobble hat and gawky patterned wellies, and she knew the names of bugs and facts about animals and nature which she could reel off with an overly earnest excitement.

We had other friends in the Troop. There weren't *cliques*, it wasn't static or forbidding: I don't want to make it seem like we were in any way divided. There was always a freedom, a fluidity, to socialising on camp. You might spend a night with people you'd never spoken to before, revealing your greatest secret just because of the fire, because of the dark – because, there together, you could trust them – we had other friends, good friends, but by the end of that week we fit together, the four of us. There was an ease.

vii.ii

THE first few hours of a camp go like this. First, everyone arrives. The leaders, who are usually there early, have made a start on setting up the main tent: a big marquee, with a power generator. If you are earlier than your friends or particularly strong, you might end up helping sit this up: occasionally parents, unwilling to leave, hang around and help. It takes a few hours to get everything in place. Benches with gas cookers run along one length of it, for cooking breakfasts and the leaders' dinners on, and carefully labelled boxes for storage. There are two plugged in freezers packed full of cheap meat and vegetables, and the rest of the food sits in giant plastic boxes: cereal, multipacks of crisps, and plastic crockery. Some of the saucepans have grotty masking tape around their handles that once marked them out for vegetarianism; at least one of them is scratchily scraped clean of its non-stick coating because Sophie infamously thought it was dirt. Last to go up are the wooden tables and benches in the middle, where everyone will eat and sit between activities, where every night you might wander over to play cards. They are stable, not too sticky, which is all you can ask of them: they're not designed for comfort.

The main tent is the heart of the camp, especially when it

rains. If it looked set to drizzle we would be told to prepare by gathering wood and storing it in our tents so we had something to cook on. I don't think anyone ever followed this incredibly sensible advice. Starting a fire with merely damp firewood is smoky and time-consuming, but possible: soaked wet wood is another matter. Still, we learnt how to use cotton wool as kindling in an emergency, and that if you could it would be a good idea to collect silver birch bark in a Quality Street tin whilst it was still dry and perfectly flammable. If these weren't options, Tony told us, you should always carry a tampon or two in any survival kit. If you tear it open, the tightly packed cotton wool makes perfect kindling. And in an emergency you can use it to help plug wounds.

Ellie and I tried to light a fire with a sanitary towel once, which wasn't as successful.

If it really poured, though, in the evening we would all have to cook on the gas grills inside the tent. Breakfast was fine: there was a routine to that, a rota that no-one could dispute. Dinner was more difficult, but it usually got done – hunger won out over pride. As a rule we cooked in small groups of four or five, dividing the tasks between us as fairly as we could. At home, I didn't really cook much, so I doubt our food was any good. It can't have been. But they were undoubtedly some of the most delicious meals of my life: spaghetti bolognaise (mince, a cruelly mistreated onion, a can of tomatoes, overboiled pasta); sweet and sour chicken, the sauce achingly sweet in jars, the rice both burnt and raw; fajitas, or veggie curry, but always plenty of carbs and a chopped vegetable or two. For what it's worth, I stand by the position I gained then that it is *impossible* to properly cook rice on a campsite. But you can get it good enough, and you'll be grateful.

If it really, really poured, we would have to lay wooden planks to act as makeshift paths between our tents and the main one. This usually became necessary anyway, as over the week the ground got beaten up, first to grass-trampled paths, then to mud. A flooded or muddy campsite is impossible to treat as if its dry. Water gets everywhere, even if you try your hardest not to let it – and there was always at least one person who'd forgotten to zip their tent up before the downpour. You adapt: learn to keep any clean, dry clothes in your sleeping bag away from the possibility of damp, learn how wet something can be before it's deemed unwearable, learn that waterproofs aren't optional but necessary, that no-one in their right mind ever camped with an umbrella, to always be wearing two pairs of socks *just in case* and to always remember where you left your hiking boots in case you need to get up in the night. (A beaten-up pair of trainers that you can slip on without having to bother with laces is also ideal.)

The second part of the camp to go up would be our

individual tents. They were meant to be 2 metres apart, for fire safety reasons, although the guy lines of next-door tents would weave in and out of each other, tantalisingly close; the tents were identical, at first, although various mishaps meant that we slowly had to replace them. One year a girl accidentally burnt a hole in ours; one year, a tent got flooded so completely it could never be used again so we turned it upside down and used it as a paddling pool.

The third part of setting up and settling in, the main part, the most exciting part, was the fire.

vii.iii

RULES for the campfire: it must never be left unattended after having just been fed; you shouldn't burn things other than wood from the assigned wood pile, especially not young, fresh, green wood, which produces more smoke than light or heat and quickly becomes rancid and overpowering; you must keep a bucket of water or two on hand at all times. I can't remember this fire bucket, which we obviously shortened to 'fucket', ever being used. There wasn't any need: the fire was vital to the camp, and however much it might be mistreated by the boys, burning plastic or porn or piss, there was understood to be a line of respect that no-one crossed. In the day, we could let it die down as we went off around the site for whatever scheduled activities we were doing.

Usually once every summer camp we'd have a full day-trip away, to a nearby seaside town, and now I can't remember how we got there. Did we have a bus? Did we walk? Did the leaders drive us in groups that would fit in their cars? The most likely option is surely that we walked, although I remember the end of those days as being limp with exhaustion, buying chips from a fish shop near a lido, which makes it seem unlikely we walked back. But not impossible.

Anyway, whatever we'd spent the day doing, come late afternoon the fire would start being stoked up again. Every night it would unwind, burning down until the last person to go to sleep covered the red embers with grey ashes overnight, so that when you came to relight it the next day the flames jumped right back. So that in one sense it was *the same fire all week*. Does Theseus's boat as a paradox apply to something that burns itself to stay alive? We treated it like a mystical being, with reverence and healthy fear. Different rules apply around a fire. It encourages connection. This is important to understand for what happened later, but also because it really was symbolic of what Scouting meant to me. When I think about our various sites at Thriftwood, they are oriented around the twin poles of the main tent and the fire: one offering as close to home comforts and domesticity as it was possible to get, the other always glimmering just out of view with something romantic and wild.

How could it have been that we never got burnt? The only serious accident I remember happened around the fire, one particularly waterlogged weekend away, but took the form of someone whittling into his thumb with a penknife. Knives were a permanent source of tension. After my first trip to Thriftwood, I told my parents I wanted one and consequently received a bright red basic Swiss Army Knife for my 12th birthday. We were required to inform the leaders that we had one, but since they were so useful for whittling the amount of kindling needed to keep a whole troop running for a week, restrictions were fairly lax. Any sign of misbehaving with a knife would get it snapped away from you almost immediately, but for general knife safety the mantra was to remember that "the pink bits are you". (I don't think at that point we did have anyone in our troop who wasn't white, though I don't know if this had occurred to TJ: as he saw it, the point of *the pink bits are you* was that it reminded you not to be a damn idiot with a blade, and if you were, well, you only had yourself to blame.) So I remember with horror Steve suddenly bursting blood all over the fire and plunging his Plath-mangled thumb into the fucket-bucket, but I don't remember any other serious injuries. TJ's view was always that if you let a bunch of kids look after themselves, they more or less would.

HOW to describe TJ? In earlier drafts of this I flirted with never naming him at all, other than by his title, *the leader*. Tony Jay. The 'Jay' surname so easily inspired shorthand nicknames: TJ, his son CJ, their respective wives Jenny and Jules, and eventually CJ's children, 'the wee-Jays'. TJ was the grizzled heart of the 26th, and he remains one of the most remarkable men I've ever met, an ill, Essex-bred King Lear in both force and tragedy. The thing that strikes me now is that he was not that old when I joined: early 60s, probably. But to my child-eyes he seemed truly ancient, in every sense of that word. His eyesight was always bad – by the time I was 18 he was basically functionally blind – and his health patchy at best. TJ was always in line for a heart operation, or needing a new walking stick, and we used to joke – except that I sorely believed it, and so did everyone else – that it was his love for Scouts, his need for us, that was the one thing that kept him going. He should have died ten times over. He was a mechanic, and until he retired from the garage we would spend some of our Troop evenings there, at least one a term. At first I hung back. Ellie always threw herself in fully, heating up random instruments in the flames to burn our initials on pieces of wood, clambering over scrap metals in search of *the perfect piece of junk,* disappearing and turning back up splattered with oil, mud, general dirt. One evening we learnt how to fix our bikes though I'm fairly sure my wobbling attempts in fact made the breaks on mine worse. We fiddled about wiring plugs properly, sawing and hammering wood into 'inventions' or 'useful camp devices'. A garage is a goldmine when you're twelve: everything is alluringly dangerous. It was by the Colchester Estuary, along a stagnant rotten stream and all the debris of a main road, and sometimes we'd be sent to litter pick around the edges of the yard and down the road. Broken bottles, crisp packets, condoms; all of us swamped in giant gardening gloves and sniggers, carefully curtailing the information we bought home to our parents: "and then TJ let us use the soldering iron, *yes* I was careful, *yes* we were supervised..."

On camps, he would tell us stories about his youth, which was so rife with danger that it seemed unbelievable and would have been instantly dismissed coming from anyone else, like the one about how, upon cutting his wrist accidentally, blood spurting everywhere like a movie, he tied it up tight, finished the job he needed to finish, and drove himself to the hospital. I was terrified of him.

I remember one early night, before I was inducted or just after, when we were outside the hut in the Garrison making some sort of go-karts. Amy and Laura, who were older, nonidentical twins, loud and brash and intimidating, persuaded me to go and ask TJ for some sandpaper. I sidled up to him and probably muttered the request.

"What??" he bellowed.

"Do you have any... sandpaper...?" (Please god don't ask me what for, I have no idea, I just do what I'm told.)

"Sandpaper?" he snorted incredulously, and probably made some kind of faux-furious, mocking comment about exactly what sort of Championship-level vehicle we thought we were building. I squeaked something out in total dismay and scampered back unsuccessfully.

The shame and fear of this encounter stayed with me for months, even when I grew to understand that TJ just was like that: brusque, a bit rough around the edges, not the sort of person to understand that the girl in front of him is standing rigid with uncalled for fear. He was kind, but it wasn't a soft kindness: he had no time for people who took the piss or didn't listen. If you wanted to come to Scouts every week and muck about for two hours, you could, but he wouldn't bother with you – all he asked was that you meet him halfway. Most people learnt. I remember sitting at dinner one camp watching the younger scouts get in trouble for not listening, as TJ shouted at them, waving his hands, lecturing. They sniggered away as if he couldn't hear – as if he was just some stupid old man trying to restrict their week of fun. After they had escaped to the fire, Ellie, Holly, a girl called Lucy and I sat with TJ and played whist. As we poured over the cards, he told us one of his stories: a motorbike accident as a teenager, his friend crashing violently. How he got up and walked forward a few metres and then, helmet still on, collapsed to the ground. Dead. I can't count how many times I heard this story, except to say that it was its repetition rather than its violence that left a mark, but now I think, *fuck*, how sad. I am glad that we listened, even if it was only sometimes, even if we rolled our eyes in private, even if we didn't realise then that just by being there we might be offering something back.

As we sat like that bats would flit round the gas lamps, drawn by the light. When I think of TJ, mostly it's of nights like that: of him pointing out the bats as Ellie made us all plastic mugs of disgustingly insipid instant hot chocolate and we played another sticky, dogeared round of whist, half-listening to an old man recount the violent death of his friend.

ix.i

THERE were terrapins in the lake at Thriftwood.

Well, allegedly. Every year I camped there someone older told me the story, until suddenly one year I was telling it too. The tale went, more or less, that a family had bought terrapins as pets (*what's a terrapin* whispered, *it's like a turtle but with teeth I think*) and that when they realized their mistake they had just released the animals into the local Scout camp lake and gone on with their lives. An alternative story was sometimes offered: that someone had taken their pet camping, smuggled in a sleeping bag, and it had escaped that way, chewed its way to freedom. The more pragmatically minded among us, on the other hand, insisted that our terrapins were *obviously* just the wild offspring of even wilder ones, marking their anger with the destruction of the planet by occasionally nibbling children's toes.

With the amount of mud in the lake, it could have been true. It was that thick, orange mud, no other word for it than *gross*, the sort that clogs your skin even just thinking about it. Nothing spa-like about this: it wouldn't do anything to your pores but suffocate them. Like the terrapins, it was always lurking at the bottom of the lake, waiting for us. We would build rafts – usually wooden planks lashed with nylon rope to four huge, plastic, chemical blue barrels – which gradually drifted apart unless we got bored and jumped off them first, hooting with success.

I wonder, often, if my muscle memory would allow me to build one of those rafts as easily as I once could. You start with a clove hitch, looping the plastic rope around a pole (if the edges start to fray, melt them back into place with a lighter), tucking the short end under to keep it in place. They're not the most stable knots, but it's the easiest way to attach a rope to a pole, and anyway, if you do the rest of it right, that shouldn't matter. It's all about keeping the tension...

You make the basic frame, like a window panel, thick round logs for the outside, smaller ones crossed inside. And then in the four compartments you've created, you can lash four big blue barrels. Sometimes we'd attach them by the handles thinking it would help for extra security, but for balance you really want to go width-wide, lashing round the top and bottom. The tighter the better: the most likely problem the raft will have is that the water will loosen the rope and the barrels will float off, at which point you might as well abandon ship.

As the rafts disintegrated, or people stopped resisting the lure of the water, the fights would kick off. Friendly but tinged with something only found in kids let loose in the woods for a week. I remember throwing people into the lake, knocking them down, reaching into the swirling water and coming back up with sick clumps of ooze to rub into a friend's protesting hair. Inevitably swallowing some of the water, spluttering horror, peeling off ruined t-shirts to expose our ungainly swimming costumes. Eventually we'd shiver our way out and head laughing up to the showers, trousers sticking to our unrecognisable monster-bodies; we'd stand under the hot taps fully dressed then eventually bundle the lake-wet clothes in a plastic Sainsburys bag at the bottom of a tent. God, how those tents must have stunk with it, the rotten water and the mud, but I don't remember any smell apart from smoke.

This whole lake escapade would usually happen twice, maybe three times in a week-long camp: rafting one day, kayaking another, zorbing, fishing, or just 'lake-side games'. Zorbing was my favourite: those giant plastic hamster-balls that you'd be sealed inside and rolled onto the water for 5 minutes of frantic running on the spot. One year we tried two-person ones, but as soon as one person lost their balance, the other person ended up crashing into them. Hilarious fun, but we suffered the bruises later. After the scheduled activities drew to an end we'd usually end up in the water anyway and always with the same result: goosepimple skin, rustorange knotted hair, someone in a huff because they'd been ganged up on. Someone else on the land dishing out the anti-bacterial hand-gel, primly, as if that could wipe out whatever bacteria we'd ingested. Showering as quickly as possible before the hot water ran out, sharing shampoo if someone had remembered to bring some. Drying off by the fire, ravenously hungry, drinking tea or instant hot chocolate and inhaling cheap, glorious biscuits until we stopped feeling the cold.

ix.ii

EVEN when I started wearing makeup to school, I never wore it on camp.

ix.iii

WHEN you're thinking things through – whatever they might be – a tent is a good place to do it in. J.L. Carr understood this. *A Month in the Country* might not be a book about camping *per se* – Thomas Birkin, the novel's narrator and protagonist does not sleep in a tent (although the quasi-archaeologist in the field next door does) but in the bell-tower of the church he is uncovering a medieval wall-painting in – but it is still about finding space outside to live, and breathe, for the new routine and practice of your life to make things visible. (I'm aware this makes it sound semi-spiritual, almost yogic, and I think there is something to be said about that similarity: for me, camping is as much about the body as is anything else, and that's not just because I tend to exercise more when I'm outside). Birkin reflects that "this steady rhythm of living and working got into me, so that I felt part of it and had my place, a foot in both present and past; I was utterly content". The routine anchors him, and there's the same attention to food and weather that appears in camping narratives. "Every day still began much alike. I brewed up, fried a couple of rashers and a round of bread and emptied my slops from the window into a nettle patch. Then I climbed down to go behind the lilac bushes (one wary eye on the scythe) and, afterwards, using Elijah Fletcher's tomb as my wash-stand, shaved."

The basic needs of the body – the lilac bushes, above which a scythe hangs on a dubiously rusty nail, is the location of a hut where Birkin has been permitted to "feel a call-of-nature" – are made routine; in doing so, Birkin is allowed to come to terms with the effects of Passchendaele and the shell-shock that forces itself onto his twitching face, with his wife leaving him for another man, having been cheating on him whilst he was fighting, with his impecunious and precarious future. These things blossom slowly in the background of a book whose basic narrative is slowly content to take things day-by-day.

Life in a country church does the same thing as life in a tent: it creates space.

Camp Two: Thriftwood, 2008

*Something in the wind has learned my name / And it's telling me
that things are not the same / In the leaves on the trees and the
touch of the breeze / There's a pleasing sense of happiness for me*

(The Carpenters, 'Top Of The World')

x

IF becoming friends with Ellie and Holly was the first
life changing experience Thriftwood gave me, the
second one came two summers later. When I seek to offer it
up, to write it so that you might understand, the best word
that comes to mind is *communion*. "Could a greater miracle
take place than for us to look through each other's eyes for
an instant?" Thoreau asks in *Walden*. That's exactly what
Thriftwood offered me, briefly, one night when I needed it
the most.

It was, I think, midweek, dusk, and Ellie and I were
lounging in the site's play area with a boy called Ben. There
was a scheduled site-wide game of manhunt going on
which we were allegedly involved in, but we were all more
interested in our own conversations. We were thirteen. A few
months ago Ben had been my first kiss: we were camping in
Mersea, playing a game of truth or dare. I had kissed three
boys that evening (three!) pretending I knew what I was
doing, showing off for attention. Afterwards Ben asked me,

softly – he is always kind when it comes to these things – if I was wearing strawberry lipgloss. I remember this vividly, not realising he was flirting with me, not realising it was a compliment: no, of course not, I said, we're on *camp*, why would I have bought make-up, I haven't even changed for two days. (In fact, I was on my period, and vividly aware that the toilets in our shitty Scout Hut didn't have any sort of bin. Too ashamed to ask anyone about this – an issue none of our male leaders had ever considered – and too afraid to test the plumbing by flushing my extra-light sanitary towels down them, I simply wrapped them tightly up and hid them in a plastic bag inside my rucksack, to be thrown away at home.)

This was not a *children's* playground, where we were perched. There was a huge tire obstacle course, the sort which rubberburns your knees, and a swing that no-one's parents would ever have let them go on, and most importantly a wooden lookout tower where the older kids made out, where sometimes there were cigarette butts, where private conversations could happen.

We were talking about puberty. Ben was the first boy I had ever talked about our bodies with. Ellie went to school with boys, so maybe she had heard it all before, but I was absolutely scandalized: they *drop*? Doesn't that *hurt*? Does it take time, or happen instantly? Could you tell straight away? All the gaps that had been left by sex education were being graphically filled in.

There were no limits to the conversation. The evening was stretching warmly and comfortably around us. At one point, a group of teenagers on the manhunt walked by with torches and we snuggled down into the tower: without having to say so, we all knew that the worst thing that could possibly happen would have been to be found, for whatever was happening between the three of us to be interrupted too early. Our words folded into each other, smooth, and suddenly we were revealing our biggest secrets to each other. It's like casting a stone into a pond. If you do it wrong, it's louder than necessary, it ripples, everyone sees; but sometimes you just know the pond will embrace it, the stone will not splash, there will be nothing to worry about. That evening, there was no danger it would go wrong.

"Alice", said Ben. "You're very quiet. What's up?" (He always asks this exactly when it was needed, it's the defining question of our friendship: *what's up, what's wrong?* He was, and remains, always unnervingly perceptive, and so kind.)

"Nothing."

"You're lying."

"I'm just thinking."

"About *someone?*" A wink, perhaps. A shadow of flirtation.

"Perhaps."

"Who?"

A decision, and then: a name.

A girl's name. The moment lingered.

The walk back to the pitch we were on that year was slow and winding. The playground is towards the very front of the campsite, past the lake and the woodpile, and we were at the back; it was far away from the road, a long walk to the shop to buy sweets, but worth it for the almost total silence at night. Having admitted what I had admitted, I was silent on the way back. You know the way your legs shake after you've exercised, or after you've had sex – the way you push your body to the limits and then it collapses into total euphoric unmoving? – that's how it felt: a trembly newness to mark the fact that, finally, someone else knew. I stared up at the trees overhead. All the anxiety of the past year since that day I'd woken up having had a dream that I'd kissed one of my school friends and thought, *perhaps I... like... girls?* seemed insubstantial. As far away a dream as civilisation. Those sorts of worries belong to houses and schools, and I knew that the woods, which were solid and real, had watched me tell Ben and Ellie, and that it would all be okay. They didn't hate me. *They didn't hate me.*

We didn't want the evening to end, any of us. We had returned because it was now properly dark and had gotten too cold to pretend otherwise, but once we'd gone back to our tents to get jumpers, we reconvened, slightly awkwardly at first. The fire was going and most of the troop was gathered around it; no doubt some of them were gossiping about us and about what could possibly be going on (did they know Ben and I had kissed? it didn't matter: Ellie and I had ditched the rest of our friends and were hanging out with a boy and being mysterious about it, which was more than enough cause for intrigue). Rather than join them, we perched on the fence in the view of the fire, warmsleepy, fluttering with the sort of human connection that only happens after dark when you're thirteen. Ellie told us a secret, something she'd never told anyone else. Ben did too. We were vulnerable. I think it was the first time I ever felt vulnerable like that, exposed but totally safe, totally willing. At their insistence I talked some more about the girl who had flooded my thoughts, how it wasn't even that I wanted to do more than just kiss her, be near her, but that something in my body was yearning in a way that I'd never felt before, that it terrified me. We shared a bar of chocolate and sat on that rickety fence until eventually the need for language dried up altogether. I could have sworn I felt the woods purr with it, the night ring with it, I could have cried with the relief and joy at having been allowed, just for one night, to breathe.

WHAT else happened that summer, the summer I came out, the summer before everything changed? My memory of the camp is mostly staccato, a series of snapshots:

1. Ellie and I make friends with a slightly older girl, Maria. She teaches us how to climb trees, revealing a wicked and energetic sense of humour. She tears her shorts on the playground as we wriggle through the tires and walks back through the camp with her underwear showing, uncaring, all of us laughing. She carries hand sanitiser with her wherever she goes and one night she walks away when a Take That song comes on through someone's shitty speakers. With the ease and intimacy of this sort of friendship, she tells us that it was played at her cousin's funeral a few weeks before, that she can't listen to it anymore. She is the first person I know my age who has lost someone not-old. We don't really stay friends after this week, at least not as intensely: it flits into the light and skips away again, painlessly, leaving no sadness.

2. It rains, and the whole troop huddles in the main tent after dinner, grumpy, and play cards. There are several decks lying about, sticky, bruised, cheap. Some people have brought their own. More people come; and soon there's almost 20 of us sharing air and a lack of space. There is no room for self-consciousness in games of cards, you'll only lose. We play cheat mostly, or a version of it mixed with slam, which involves whacking your hand down on a pile of cards as quickly as you can. Imagine ten, fifteen bodies hurling themselves onto a rickety, wet table, exhilarated. Usually a little bruised.

3. Kyle practises dealing cards in multiple ways, some more successful than others: one particularly flamboyant attempt leaves them scattered all over the grass and my stomach aching with laughter.

4. Holly and I skive off one of the activities, or leave early, and cut our way back through the campsite. When we get there, we're met by a squirrel who has got into the box of supplies and opened a screwtop jar of peanut butter, and doesn't even

look embarrassed about it, despite being caught peanut-handed. He scampers away eventually, but with a sort of resignation – well, if I *must*. We debate whether or not to throw the peanut butter away. I can't remember what we decide.

5.   Two couples form, and fight, and kiss by the fire.

6.   Trundling out of the water on one of those lakedays, we discover the bonding experience of being *teenage girls*, separate creatures, marked. Hormones, sleeping and eating and living together: wake up, surprise, you've all *synced. That's real? I didn't think it was real. But no, I heard Laura is on too, that makes five of us – and I wasn't due on for a week – wow I wonder when I'll be that regular.* I had barely started having my period, it was only a few months before that I'd noticed the streak of blood in my bikini, left it for a few hours whilst I went about my day and then, deciding that yep, this was probably *it*, offhandedly told my mum in the bathroom at Zizzis. I didn't have the habit of planning for this yet, and it seemed like no-one else on the camp had either.

What to do? We fence ourselves off from the boys in prickly solidarity and confer. Whispering to each other, *does anyone have?* – but no one bought enough pads or tampons with them for everyone. Suddenly the fact that all the leaders, especially TJ, are men is a problem, in a way it has never been before, not ever. That, more than anything, feels unsteady. We eventually secure a supply and sidle in clusters to the toilets where, outraged with the unfairness of it all, Lucy runs forward and shouts into the men's bathroom: *WE HATE WINGS*!! To annoy them, maybe, or confuse them with a code they have no access to – and if they somehow do, to at least gross them out. I don't have any opinion on *wings* or really know what they are, but I know that it's not the wings we hate, not really, it's the sudden difference between us. The branching of a line.

That night and for the rest of the week we all fold tissue paper into our underwear and pretend it's fine.

7. A group of Scouts from Nigeria are camping opposite us. They spent the week before at the Essex International Jamboree in Chelmsford and are extending their trip with a week here. As I walk past one day, they call me over and we chat. A girl named Blessing braids my hair and says I look

73

beautiful, and we exchange emails; years later, I will add her on Facebook, where she will stoically like all my selfies for years. We will remain a tangential half-remembered part of each other's lives.

8. The site has a group-wide campfire once a week – Thursday nights, usually, though that's weather dependant – and we all go along. Some of the Guides on site bring blankets, which we mock them for, even though it can get *so* cold waiting for it to start. You have to choose your seat wisely: too close by the fire, the heat is immense. Too far and you get no warmth. The songs vary in quality. A man sits next to Sarah and rams into her hard during the jostling part of 'we're going on a bearhunt', and she insists it was done on purpose. Ellie, Maria and I change the words to 'I am a music man': *what can you play? I play... the harmonica: blow suck blow suck blow, blow suck blow, blow suck blow* – until we are all crying rebellious tears of laughter and people are scowling at us. But as the fire draws to a close I draw myself off from my friends, knowing I will cry during *Kum-ba-yah* even though I am not religious. It always makes me cry.

I think softly that if I did have a god, it would be

this: sitting outside in the night lit up with flames and all of my friends, singing together, the fire slowly burning down, and no set bedtime.

9. No-one shits on the fire this year, or at least, no-one is seen doing so.

xii

JACK London's *The Call of the Wild* was first published in 1903. It opens with an epigraph, the first stanza of a poem called 'Atavism' by John Myers O'Hara:

> Old longings nomadic leap,
> Chafing at custom's chain;
> Again from its brumal sleep
> Wakens the ferine strain.

The rest of the poem resounds with a call to nature:

> Helots of houses no more,
> Let us be out, be free-;
> Fragrance through window and door
> Wafts from the woods, the sea.
>
> ...
>
> Temple thy dreams with the trees,
> Nature thy god alone;
> Worship the sun and the breeze,
> Altars where none atone.

It is not particularly good verse, but it is striking, coming as it does from that moment of the beginning of the twentieth century when the gold rush to which Jack London would be so drawn was getting underway. *Temple thy dreams with the trees*. It is fitting for my copy of *The Call of the Wild*, which was a book I developed a strange attachment to at around the age of ten. Strange because it was so powerful and so, apparently, random – I picked up the book for 20p at a charity stall and read it, reread it, treasured it. I was obsessed with wolves at the time – I was writing a 'novel', a loose adaptation of *The Lord of the Rings* with a cursed amulet and a pack of four brave wolves, seeking to destroy it to prevent the evil centaurs from getting their hooves on it – and something about the language, the plot, the drawings in my copy, all came together and I fell in love. Just as with a person, when you fall in love with a book, it doesn't have to be reasonable, it might never make sense.

I took my copy with me on every camp I went on, even when I no longer needed to read it to call up huge swathes of the text. I have it next to me now: stained yellow with spilt shampoo, bent in half, it's definitely been rained on more than once. The book tells the story of Buck, a great 'tide-water dog, strong of muscle and with warm, long hair' stolen from a family in Santa Clara and sold by their desperate gardener as a sled-dog 'since men, groping in the Arctic darkness, had found a yellow metal'. He comes to lead a pack of huskies but then is sold to inexperienced travellers who work him beyond his strength; a kind man rescues him, understands his value, and nurses Buck back to health. He is tempted away by the wild towards which his nature yearns, but his love for the man keeps drawing him back; when he is eventually killed, Buck is released from the ties of men and leaps into the wolfpack. It is an essential, instinctive view of nature – there is a scene early on where Buck, lying by the fire, seems to see something like a past life, like the whole history of canine domestication:

> Sometimes as he crouched there, blinking dreamily at the flames, it seemed that the flames were of another fire, and that as he crouched by this other fire he saw another and different man [...] This other man was shorter of leg and longer of arm, with muscles that were stringy and knotty rather than rounded and swelling. The hair of this man was long and matted, and his head slanted back under it from the eyes. He uttered strange sounds, and seemed very much afraid of the darkness, into which he peered continually, clutching in his hand, which hung midway between knee and foot, a stick with a heavy stone made fast to the end. He was all but naked, a ragged and fire-scorched skin hanging part way down his back, but on his body there was

much hair. In some places, across the chest and shoulders and down the outside of the arms and thighs, it was matted into almost a thick fur. He did not stand erect but with trunk inclined forward from the hips, on legs that bent at the knees. About his body there was a peculiar springiness, or resiliency, almost catlike, and a quick alertness as of one who lived in perpetual fear of things seen and unseen. At other times this hairy man squatted by the fire with head between his legs and slept. On such occasions his elbows were on his knees, his hands clasped above his head as though to shed rain by the hairy arms. And beyond that fire, in the circling darkness, Buck could see many gleaming coals, two by two, always two by two, which he knew to be the eyes of great beasts of prey. And he could hear the crashing of their bodies through the undergrowth, and the noises they made in the night. And dreaming there by the Yukon bank, with lazy eyes blinking at the fire, these sounds and sights of another world would make the hair to rise along his back and stand on end across his shoulders and up his neck, till he whimpered low and suppressedly, or growled softly, and the half-breed cook shouted at him, "Hey, you Buck, wake up!" Whereupon the other world would vanish and the real world come into his eyes, and he would get up and yawn and stretch as though he had been asleep.

It is made clear that Buck's talent, such as it is, lies in his ability to get to grips with his instincts quickly. It's a uncomfortable philosophy lying side by side, as it does, with the tendency of Scouting history, and similar groups, to skirt eugenics. Matthew De Abaitua in *The Art of Camping* and Elleke Boehmer in her introduction to *Scouting for Boys* are both excellent on this. The former writes that

> If we are to celebrate the simple pleasures of camping, that feeling of being close to the land, the unspoken but palpable sense of community, the camper's exultation in doing rather than passively consuming, then we must consider the monstrous iteration of those ides in Germany from the beginning of the twentieth century to Hitler's assumption of the role of chancellor in 1933.

It is not just the Nationalism that runs through the Scouting movement, and Baden-Powell's own brush with Nazism, that is to be interrogated, but the way camping itself seems to encourage a similar response to the natural world. London's racism is clear but covert here – in his references to the 'half-breed' cook (a Scotsman) – but his is still fundamentally less an *adapting* than an un-adapting; a growing back to the past.

A knowing, innately, what to do, what it all means, where you belong. It can be abused. 'Nature thy god alone'... but we did feel it, on camp, feel something inside us waking up that we barely knew had been asleep.

Camp Three: Thriftwood, 2010

I will always remember / that first stolen moment ('Bare', from the
soundtrack of *Bare: A Pop Opera*)

xiii

SHE *sits by the fire all limbs and frantic, silly energy, and holds his hand. She will regret this moment* a million times over. *When she looks back, she will wonder how she didn't spot it: the world shifting around her, the earth groaning from her entrails, her own private fall. A name with a serpent's hiss and a cocky grin and how with all his attention focussed on you, you could melt. That's why. Who has time for omens, for foresight, when those eyes.*

The woods take on a charge they never had before. Every tree is alive with it. She wants to kiss him. She has barely kissed anyone before: Ben, yes, and a boy on a campsite family holiday in France who wouldn't leave her alone afterwards. They made out in the French showers, and he left her disgusted and frightened. But this boy...

She thinks, briefly, of Lucy. Touching the wound, seeing how it feels in this company. It feels like a betrayal, which is ridiculous. But still, the memory pangs. Maybe it always does, thinking of the first person who makes you so aware of the movement of your body.

She came expecting a week of shattered glass softness, pretending never to see her, bones on edge, and then she did not come, although she had promised, weeks ago, in passing, thoughtless words that caused a vibration, a vibration that here came to its juddering close. He bats her words away, reveals them to be the insubstantial dust they always were. She feels stupid for having cared so very much.

The trees groan. She feels like an adult. She recognises their moans and misinterprets them. She holds his hand. The woods are crying screaming pleading. From the future, telling this story, I close my eyes in resignation.

IT is summer 2010 and the girl I deeply, desperately fancy is not at Thriftwood like she said she would be.

I don't blame her for what happened there. I don't blame anyone except the two of us: him, and me. But I do remember, at the start of that camp, feeling hurt that she wasn't there and moulding my decisions out of that hurt. She had *said* she was going to be there, in passing, by the vending machine at school.

As a school, we were obsessed with lunch. At 12:30 about 200 girls would *sprint* towards the canteen. And I mean sprint: we would start edging towards the door of our form rooms, or practise timing our entrances to be seated as close to the doors in assembly as possible, before hurtling our way out on release, leaping down stairs, straining for the front of the queue, a pack of wild animals. It must have been so dangerous – miraculously there was only ever one semi-serious accident – but the difference between the back of the queue and the front was not only about 20 minutes of precious lunch wasted but also a serious dent to your pride. Eventually, this flood of running teenage girls – racing for a supply of food which was never in danger of running out – was officially quelled and running in the corridors strictly forbidden.

Still, I remember the pang of getting there, out-of-breath, starving, and my first instinct being to look round the room, to see if *she* was already sat and eating with friends. If she was I would blush bright red and the friends I had confided in would give me knowing glances, understanding that it meant I had seen her and my heart was racing. After Ben and Ellie, it became easier and easier to say it out loud, until I had told almost everyone, although without letting any of them know it was no longer technically a secret at all. Some friends I told over text, some in person, choking it out or hinting at it, flirting at it, hiding the words under my tongue or whispering them into the stream of secret ichor that fed our friendships. I was not the first person in our class to come out, but I was the first person who wasn't desperately uncool and unliked, whose sexuality wasn't another weapon to levy against them, so it still felt like mapping new ground: there was no telling who might care.

For two years, I craved her. I remember almost every conversation I ever had with her. I memorised the moments when her timetable clashed with mine and made sure to give myself the maximum possible chance of bumping into her. Wednesdays were the best and the worst days: in the morning, we had lessons in neighbouring classrooms; in the afternoon we had PE at the same time, and I had to change inches away from her, my skin and soul burning, terrified I might accidentally glance in her direction, desperately aware of her presence. Even sweeter were the moments where we met unexpectedly: when she once (I shook for hours afterwards) stopped me in the corridor and asked if I'd be at Explorers that evening, then asked me what I was up to. Or when I went to the vending machine one lunchtime and she told me she'd be on summer camp.

I thought my heart might break at the thought. A whole week in a proximity so scalding; everyone who knew laughing at me; my desperate, clumsy attempts at friendship, at being in her presence, at knowing where she was at all times so I could safely, miserably, yearn. I could barely look at her: eye contact was searing. How could I survive a week?

I told her of my feelings once, over text. It was snowing. She didn't have my number. I got hers off our leader the night before, making up some excuse for needing it, and sent her a poem. She thought it was a joke.[1] I was tobogganing with my mum and my sister when she finally replied with confusion, a touch of laughter. How else was she to take a sudden confession of desire when I had hidden my interest beneath rudeness for almost two years, scowling so she didn't see my heart beating in my eyelids?

So whilst I counted down the days until a week together,

---

1   In fairness, the poem ended in the atrocious couplet "every breath that I take echoes your name / if you smiled at me nothing would ever be the same", so I don't hold it against her that she wasn't as bowled over as I'd hoped.

in the end she didn't come to Thriftwood, and probably never once thought about that decision, and so when one evening a group of us were invited over to the campsite next door, I went. Ellie and Sarah thought the whole idea was stupid. They told me not to go, but I was drunk with something – dizzy with the thrill of acting out, with ditching my friends for the unknown alternative. With promise, maybe. Fate. Bitterness at having been shown, yet again, how all the things I didn't ever actually think would happen with Lucy, regardless of what I whispered into my diary at night, really never would. What did I think, I chastised myself – that our eyes and hands and hearts would meet over the tentpoles, that we'd build a raft together and she'd realise we were meant to be together?

That evening, I met Max.

xv.i

IT was dusk and we were singing.

The other campsite's fire was less good than ours. At the start, at least I was not so entranced that I failed to notice *that*. We sat round it awkwardly: four of us, all girls, seven or so of them, all boys. They were drinking, which we never did. At least, I don't remember anyone ever mentioning alcohol, even suggesting it, even people who drank, but it is possible – maybe even likely – that I was just oblivious. Everyone on the other site was also underage, but there didn't appear to be any leaders in sight anywhere. This was totally unlike our camp, where our leaders mingled with us like equals. But the flipside of that, I supposed, was this freedom: beers, boys, the taste and tension of suddenly feeling teenage. There was technically nothing stopping us from doing this – hanging out at someone else's camp, making friends with strangers, unsupervised. But it felt frowned upon, somehow inherently rebellious.

At one point the fire was overrun by children, who – without the benefit of acquaintance – were even more annoying than the cubs and beavers we'd left behind. By this point, I was feeling pretty awkward. My mind had fluttered back to its own private sorrow and I was wondering why

I hadn't just gone with Ellie and Sarah, or if I'd ever learn how to make conversation, how to joke and be light. At least there was the fire to look at. With a fire going, you don't have to make eye contact with anyone: it's okay to be silent. Especially if there's no-one to make eye contact with. Some boy had started flirting with a girl from our site, and she flipped her hair, confident, and flirted back. I caught myself staring at the two of them resentfully: it seemed so easy and natural to her. If only I could talk to *her* like that. At least then we could be friends, at least she wouldn't think I was arrogant in my silence, or, worse, disinterested – maybe she'd even realise she was thinking about me more and more and ask me to hang out, or...

Was I already sitting next to him at that point? How did we start talking?

I don't know. I don't even know when I first noticed him as more than a stranger. But when the younger boys flooded in, loud and irritating, I know that we looked at each other in pissed-off recognition. He had long, floppy hair, always artfully arranged, and a cheap iPod knock off. And then he offered me an earbud: us and music against the children.

And maybe my skin brushed his as I took it. Maybe not. I was too embarrassed to comment truthfully on his music, which was unlike anything I could have expected: a mixture of musicals (good), classical piano (confusing) and furious, mostly German, heavy metal (bad). He curled in soft to talk about them into my ear, even when the crowd quietened down; I listened to him rhapsodising every band, nodded, pretended I understood. His breath smelt like the lager I had never drunk and at some point he took my hand.

Originally, I wrote that I took his. I wish that were true. But I think, if I am being honest, that he must have been the one who reached over, who initiated things. I think that I would never have been brave enough.

A tree cracked. The fire dimmed. He held my hand and we listened to music.

Eventually, a leader came to get us. We were told to go back to our own campsite now, firmly but politely. My skin was fire-licked-burning, I was desperate with it. He said quietly to me, alone, *come back tomorrow*, a command not a request and I said almost without knowing it *I will*.

When I got back I realised I didn't know his full name, but I rolled what I had in my mouth like a sweet: Max. Max. Max.

xv.ii

Ihave tried so hard to make people understand how it happened, how that first night by the fire bathed everything that was to follow in flickering, beautiful, untrustworthy flames. I don't know if the details I remember – all those jagged bits of glass – help or detract from that. I have rewritten the above scene hundreds of times: in diaries, emails, conversations. Do I *need* to mention the metal music? Should I insist on his habit of bursting into song at any given moment, make it clear just how much that characterised conversation with him? Would it make people understand, at last, if I finally got the formula right, was able to perfectly put into words how I felt? He was entrancing. I was entranced.

I thought I was a bad writer for years because nothing I sent to him or wrote for him changed his mind. Is that same impulse at work here? I want so, so desperately to know that you can *see* it: a shy girl, an extroverted, mature boy. The fire. The cold air drawing us all in towards each other. The uncomfortable camping chairs and Fleur smirking because she's seen we're holding hands and the future hanging wide open. Cavernously open. I imagine the trees warning me in a silent stream of consciousness, a proleptic scream: *you have understood the love and wonder that runs through this place, we*

have given it to you, we love you, we love you, but this heat you are
feeling is not our love, this heat is the wrong sort, stop.

I don't think any of these details matter, at least not to people who can be objective. They don't care. Maybe you don't care. But maybe if I bombard you with them, the way they seared through me, you might understand how it took over every cell until something changed. You might understand why it was that I allowed him to destroy my life.

The more real Max is, the more I paint him as I saw him then, the harder it becomes to reconcile the truth about what he did. His reality flickers, too. How can he have been a teenage boy who collected horror films, who lived for musical theatre, who could quote whole episodes of *Friends,* who drank caramel lattes, who wasn't very good at kayaking? How can I hold that reality alongside the other reality, let alone hold both of those alongside my very real love for him?

xv.iii

WHAT happens to your love for someone when they do something wrong? It becomes both true and untrue. That line of Anne Carson's:

> "You remember too much,
> my mother said to me recently.
> Why hold onto all that? And I said,
> Where can I put it down?"

blurs into Cordelia in Evelyn Waugh's *Brideshead Revisited*, who has "no past tense of the verb to love". God, but that feels like an accusation.

To love always in the present like Cordelia is a kind of trauma. In the same way that PTSD arises when you fail to adequately process a traumatic event, loving someone who is abusive or cruel freezes your love. It makes a mockery of it. Because you cannot *stop loving them* on demand, not even if you want to. Not even if you know you should.

First you must reconcile the fact that the person you loved did something terrible – *whilst* you loved them and *despite the fact* you loved them. Only then can you learn where to put that love down, how to write it into the past tense. You must learn that even if your relationship was abusive – even if you were lied to so that what you thought was real never existed – your *love* itself was not bad.

What I mean is: loving people is not bad.

No, that's not what I mean. What I mean is it is okay for me to say, for example, 'I loved him' *and to no longer love him*. If you believe that conditional love, love that ends, is somehow fake, *that's* when you can never put it down.

For years, I thought if I *stopped* loving him it would mean that I *never* loved him at all; that I was lying whenever I promised myself (and him) that I would love him forever.

What I mean is, I have gone back to that scene by the fire for years and years and years begging myself not to take his hand, but that was just another way of keeping the love alive. I no longer wish I hadn't done it. What good would it do?

So, yes, I loved him, I won't deny that any more, I won't pretend to rewrite it.

xv.iv

FOR the year after that night I told the story time and time again, rewriting into a funny, scandalous thing to drop into drinking games or flirtations. The truth is that the next day, the day after the fire, I was absurdly scared I wouldn't recognise him. It felt like a dream; I couldn't picture him in the light.

We went over to the lake to kayak that afternoon and their troop was there too. I felt myself blushing in my designated muddy water clothes and life jacket, I felt myself suddenly deeply uncool. Desperate for his attention, alternating between being too loud and too silent, showing off, splashing my friends, wondering if he was looking yet, and if so, was he looking at me? When eventually we made eye contact he smirked noncommittally. I wondered if he'd forgotten about the promise of a plan between us. In all my anxiety about what I'd do that evening, how far I'd be willing to go, it never once crossed my mind that maybe *he* wouldn't be interested. Maybe he'd found someone else, someone less awkward, someone who wasn't wearing ripped waterproof trousers and an old stained jumper. Someone who knew what they were doing. How to flirt, how to be sexy.

Whatever had fractured that first night by the fire, I was

desperate for it, counting down the hours until we could go back over. Of course I recognised him. My blood was already screaming for him (Max, Max, Max). Ellie teased me about it but with an edge of derision that seemed new. This wasn't like my toothless, longing crush on Lucy: this could hurt us all. Fleur treated me with a fascination she'd never shown before, linking arms with me, pulling me to sit with her and her boyfriend. The two of them – in between making out with each other – asked me about the boy I was with, *your boy* I think Fleur said, and I felt an amazed, possessive pride, that there was something in the world that tied someone like him to someone like me. Even if it was just an accident of grammar; even if he'd changed his mind.

The afternoon trickled by until, suddenly, it was dark. We went over after dinner. I was hypernervous. Fleur was teasing. Max was waiting for me. We sat, along with everyone else, by the fire, whispering to each other, skirting round the edge of the precipice, waiting, waiting, waiting. When the appropriate amount of time had passed (minutes, hours? Max was the timekeeper, he knew how this played out – I was just breathing, fizzing into nerve endings, his hand in my hand, each touch jarringly new) he pulled me up. Led me to his tent.

NOTE: I did not lose my virginity in a tent. Not that tent or any other.

Note: I never had penetrative sex with Max. It matters, because to have done so would have mattered. I don't think much of the concept of virginity but I know that sex with Max would have changed something.

xv.vi

WE kissed, of course. For all that I remember about the build-up to that evening, I remember surprisingly little about what took place. I know I took my necker off, my shirt, my bra. I had never done anything like this, let alone with a stranger. I had never kissed anyone lying down, never pressed my body against someone like I was testing myself. He was totally in charge. But – don't get me wrong – I was enthralled. I wanted it, I wanted him. I thought, *he must really like me*. I thought, *no one at school would believe this*. I thought, *I don't really believe this, I only met him yesterday*.

Later, when things were at their worst, I used to tell Em that Max would *never be able to rape me*, because I always wanted to have sex with him. Why did I think that was a normal, unworrying thing to say? But there was a truth to it, a truth that coursed through every interaction we had: that I wanted him somewhere deep down, somewhere essential.

I don't know what might have happened that night, because someone came to get me, in a panic: the leaders were looking for me.

xv.vii

BECAUSE I am interested in memory, and the way we reconstruct our past, I feel confessed to admit: I lied, just now. The truth is, we did not sneak into his tent straight away. We sat by the fire, and flirted, and then – just like the night before – Julie, CJ's wife, the only woman on that camp, came to get me.

"Come back", he told me, again. I never even thought about disobeying. So we said our goodnights, kissed goodbye ostentatiously, and I walked back with Julie and the others, waited a suitably decent amount of time, and then told Fleur the plan. She would help smuggle me through the woods to his campsite; she'd keep an eye out for me in case my absence was noticed. It would be an adventure. And it was so romantic! Of course she agreed. She snuck me through the woods, even though it started to rain, even though we could hear Julie's voice ringing loud behind us, reminding us that this was a transgression of the sort I'd never made before. But we made it back to their camp. Illicitly. *That's* when Max took my hand and pulled me to his tent. I'd proved myself, I guess. I'd made my choice clear.

A fracture ran between me and the leaders for the first time. The thrill of active disobedience.

xvi.i

SO, there we were, kissing and undressing in the dark. And then one of his friends – possibly called Dan, or Dave? – hissed through the tent flap: "Alice – they're looking for you!" Fuck, oh fuck. Practically a full blown search party. Luckily the night was overcast, stormscaled sky. I dressed quickly. We kissed goodbye. I ran back through the woods, heart pounding: at my core, I am not a rule-breaker.

Fleur was frantic. She'd told Julie that I'd gone to the toilet, that she was overreacting, that *of course* I hadn't gone back to that boy's site. Jules knew me, didn't she? *Alice wouldn't do that.* I snuck by the campsite towards the direction of the toilets, then turned around to double back on myself, so that I approached the camp casually, sauntering: oh, what, you were all looking for me? I was just in the toilet. I felt sick. I was brushing my teeth. How long had you been looking?

No-one believed me, of course. No-one would make eye contact with me. For the first time that night, I understood how sex can cut the world apart.

The next day felt heightened. Like all the colour in the world was there: everywhere else must have been bled dry. Everyone seemed to be whispering about me – maybe they'd all heard me and the others giggling in the tent the night before as I regaled everyone with a story of my *adventure*. That was the night that seven of us slept in one tent: it got so hot we had to unzip the tent flap, we were so squashed in no-one could move, lying across each other's limbs and clothes like dolls. It remains one of the best night's sleep I've ever had, pressed against my friends. Soft. There was none of the ferocity I'd had earlier, lying against Max. Instead I felt secure, moored in a world that was changing beyond all recognition. Julie might have suspected me but we'd never gotten on that well anyway. It would be okay.

I sat down with Ben at breakfast the next morning and there was a look in his eyes I'd never seen. "I heard you're in trouble", he said, and there wasn't anything malicious in it but for the first time it was the voice of a boy talking to a girl. All the closeness of the summer before recoiled into nothingness.

Sometime later that day Julie took me aside for a *talk*. About responsibility, and how on camp *we are responsible for you*; they wouldn't tell my parents, but I can't go over there again, *do you understand?* I stared at the ground silently cheekburningfurious. *You have never felt anything like this,* I wanted to say. *The way he looked at me.* Maybe if I'd said it – what? She might have understood then that I had no idea what I was doing, that I was falling out of my depth, gasping? She might have understood how essentially vulnerable I was to someone like him? Maybe if she'd told my parents what had happened everything afterwards would have been different. But then, if *I'd* told my parents... Of course, I never considered it. I couldn't. That would have damaged the sanctity of camp: this space was not for them. Thriftwood was ours.

Max would never have looked at me anywhere else.

I thought I knew the way this all worked, where things like desire fitted in. But suddenly it seemed both too huge and too small, like I was shifting slightly out of focus: nothing seemed real apart from my want for Max. When you've never felt either before, it's easy to mistake *want* for *love*, concern for oppression. Julie said she'd talked to his leaders, that they were going to be keeping an eye on him for the rest of the week, just as she was going to be keeping an eye on me. I hated her for that: how dare she embarrass me in front of him? How dare she act as if this was anything other than the greatest intrusion?

I wonder, now, what they told her about him.

xvi.ii

JULIE must have sensed that she wasn't really getting through to me, because that evening, Tony also asked to talk to me.

It was truly excruciating: even now I feel it twist cold in my gut. The fucking awkwardness of it. Something like this had never really happened before and everyone wanted to know, afterwards, what he'd said. He was never afraid to publicly call out scouts for their misdemeanours: if you were stupid, foolish, careless, he would let you know. That was part of the deal. Taking me aside, dealing with me privately, was the loudest possible way he could tell everyone how much trouble I was in.

Unlike the aftermath of my telling off from Julie, which saw me spewing vitriol behind her back in the way only a teenager can – *bitch*, I said, *she's just jealous, she doesn't know what she's talking about* – I had absolutely no desire to recount my conversation with TJ to anyone. It was not just that I was deathly embarrassed – although he was old enough to be my grandfather, far too old to be talking to me about sex – but the disappointment he showed in me was devastating. He did not pretend to be my friend. He simply showed the steel at the heart of things, made me understand that there was an authority in our relationship that could be bought to bear on me if I made it necessary. That all the freedoms I'd assumed intrinsic to Thriftwood could be taken away if I showed myself unworthy.

Back in the tent, eyes stinging (I have never been able to take being told off by anyone I respect without crying) I turned my phone on to see if my parents were checking in. I had a text from Max: *come to my tent :)*. I replied explaining the situation, apologising. He didn't say anything. I checked my phone, obsessively, waiting for him to reply, no longer trying to conserve battery, just desperate to hear something.

Two days later, his dad died.

xvi.iii

MAX and his friends came over in the middle of the day, a little drunk (although I'm not sure anyone but me picked up on that); he bowed to Julie, I think, obsequiously asked her permission to go with me to the lake. His leaders must have said something else to her because she agreed at once. He charmed her – he could charm anyone, flirt with anyone, his confidence and delight at doing so always seeped through – but I was less easily soothed. Delight at seeing him was coloured by the sudden realisation that I was nervous. Beyond the shadows of a night-time fire, would he find me at all interesting? Would I be attractive in the daylight?

I took two chocolate minirolls in my pocket to give my hands something to do and we wandered down to the lake. Once there, I didn't know what to say; I ate chocolate silently, sickly, and offered him a bite. He took it out of my hands and threw it into the lake. I watched it bobbing in the water pathetically and said something nonsensical about littering that broke the tension. At last, we kissed. Then, his arm around me, we talked.

He unhooked the silver teardrop shaped necklace I always wore and put it round his own neck. In the light for the first time, I saw that his arms were criss-crossed with cuts. He told me he was depressed. It impressed me: mental illness hadn't wormed its way into my conscience much before, aside from a friend at school who would threaten suicide, cut themselves after PE lessons with a maths compass. (A friend and I took the compass off him and told an English teacher we trusted; no-one really bothered following it up with us, although he diligently went off to the flimsy school-offered counselling every week for a term or so. And I never said anything to my parents. Like who fancied who or who was arguing with who, it never seemed like their place to know. All secrets were kept on an equal footing; I had no way of distinguishing between them.)

My bodywarm jewellery glittering on his t-shirt, Max finally told me he was going home early. Back to Sussex. It seemed a world away. I didn't know what to say: how could any of *this*, this next-to-nothing thing, possibly continue in the outside world? It seemed as much part of Thriftwood as cooking on an open fire did, as sleeping in full clothes and eating a fried breakfast every morning and playing cards in the rain did. None of these things belonged to my life outside; how could Max? Those were the rules. But, god, I wanted him to stay, I wanted to embrace him into the rest of my life.

Why are you going home early?

Well. My mum called. She didn't say. But my dad has terminal cancer. He's – he's probably dying. Or dead.

I didn't know anyone with cancer either. It was as adult

as the kissing and the self-harm: sex and love all twisted up with hatred and death. He let me kiss his scars as he told me I was beautiful and that he loved me, that of course we'd stay in contact, and he cried in my arms as we held each other, and we sat by the lake like that intertwined, and he said he *needed* me. *Me.*

And then he left for the hospital, still wearing my necklace. Julie, TJ and the others treated me cautiously, kindly: it was obvious I was devastated. I'd gone from being good and well-behaved to scandalous and slutty to quasi-bereaved, all in the space of a week. And I was so worried for him. My phone had, finally, run out of power so I had to wait until I got home on Saturday to text him.

When I did, I carefully wrote his name in full in my diary, along with a record of the week's events. I thought, otherwise, I might forget it.

xvii

THE last hours of a camp are always a strange limbo. Dismantling tents that have come to seem like home means suddenly revealing the campsite in all its smallness. Crumpled yellow grass where your beds have been. The main tent, so unshakable and safe throughout storms and sun alike, was suddenly trussed up in TJ's car and the fire spluttered out; we ate the last scraps of food and could no longer measure the hours ahead of us as if they were endless. Time seeped back into shape. That year, Ellie's dad drove the three of us back, exhausted and grotty. I remember the car journey vividly; the homesick sinking feeling increasing the further away we got, the way every story we related about what we'd been up to seemed to have a gaping hole in it. When I got home and my parents asked how the week had been, I could barely think of anything to say. Sitting naked in a filthy bath, washing off the accumulated grime off the week, I wondered if he was thinking of me. More than anything, I wondered if he was okay.

His dad died on Friday. I can't remember if the funeral was before or after he came to see me: after, I should think. I do remember that I didn't know what to do about his grief – was I meant to say something? Or was I there to act as a distraction?

I was shakingly nervous, fizzing with it. My mum had an old schoolfriend and her sons staying and they'd gone out for the day, so the house was empty. I excused myself from the trip with the casual mention that I was meeting up with someone from Scouts, purposefully not giving too much detail. I rang a friend from school on the way to the train station and she gave me directions over the phone because I'd only ever been driven there before. It took me about forty minutes to walk there, but I made it, several wrong turnings later (I have always had a terrible sense of direction) and, probably, overdressed, overcompensating; clumsy blue eyeliner all around my eyes and a palpable sense of uncertainty. He liked me on camp: would he like me in the real world, too?

And then he was there.

I took him into town, tripping over my words, my feet, showing off, desperate to make him like it, like me, desperate – already – to give him some happiness, to forge a link in his mind between joy and me. I showed him the high street and overexplained everything until he pointed out softly that he did in fact know what a Superdrug was. We looked at makeup together – I'd never met a boy who wore makeup before – and then we went to Costa –

It feels so *small,* laying it all out like this. It's not like I hadn't done the same thing time and time again with my friends: pottering round the shops, spending money we didn't really have or cheap tops from New Look and makeup we were still learning how to use from Boots; gossiping over too sugary coffee drinks, sharing cakes, huddled round sticky franchise tables for hours, laughing too loudly. I lived within easy walking distance to the town, and my school was a short walk away too, so it wasn't like it was new or exciting to be doing what we were doing. It was just that doing it with him made everything different. It felt airless. Alien. Like the world had been flooded, and then electrocuted, until all my nerves were buzzing with stimulation. Like I had been opened up, that his grief and lust and the secrets he had told me were all laser weapons aimed at what normality had been, that they had exploded the world and now, here I was, a sparked eel swimming through the rubble, feeding off it, off the total and utter shock of it all.

(Anne Carson again:

> They were two superior eels
> at the bottom of the tank and they recognised each
> other like italics.)

We ran into a girl I vaguely knew at one point, and although normally we'd have said hi and let it go, I felt myself become different. An object of interest – is that *Alice*, with a *boy*? It wasn't just that I wanted to show him off to the world. I felt his desire for me thickening, becoming a new sense of self-worth. If someone like *this* wanted me – someone cool, beautiful, someone who drank and didn't care what adults think, and who, crucially, was so, so sad – then I wasn't just the girl who did well at school and read a lot and was quiet and secretly boring. I was better than that.

All of which is to say that even his coffee order – a large caramel latte with an extra shot of espresso – impressed itself on my mind; that for years later, I would associate coffee with him as if it was a sign. (As if drinking coffee was a character attribute; as if it meant anything at all.) And after the coffee, he took my hand – finally – and we walked back to mine, as if it was entirely natural, as if this was what every cell in my body had been waiting for since the moment I'd met him. Which perhaps it was.

xviii

HE *takes off his shoes by the door and they look alien, hilariously large, out of place. And maybe she offers him a tea out of nervousness. Maybe he accepts out of kindness.*

They lie together in a small single bed. A child's bed, still. A lavender coloured room, with a matching duvet cover embroidered with a smiling, shell-clad mermaid. An embarrassing room. The clutter of being fifteen. Definitively not a sexy room. Tidy, because it always was, and because she cleaned for him. As if he'd care.

He says, how far have you gone? *Attempting to sound cool and grown up, she says· this. She hopes he thinks that she means she has done this before with others rather than the truth, which is that everything he does to her, everywhere he touches, is new. He sparks newness, makes her arch with newness.*

He lies on top of her and they kiss. She starts to understand what friction can do. After he has finished touching her he moves his body catlike down, kisses her softly, flicks his tongue –

When he is done, or when she is done, he raises his head. She is in ecstasy.

She pretends not to notice his eyes are red with tears.

xix.i

I knew then, I think. That we were telling ourselves different stories about it. But I shut that thought out. My family came home, saving me from his suggestions of reciprocation and from me having to admit that I had never seen a dick before and didn't know what to do, that this was all frighteningly new. My mum drove us to the station as Taylor Swift's *Love Story* played over the radio and she pretended not to notice we were holding hands. That evening, as punishment for whatever line I had crossed – and she never asked, never thought to say it out loud – I had to take my sister and a friend to the cinema. Some vacuous summer movie played and I curled up on my own delight, my desperately beating heart, my secret thrill, waiting only until I was alone in bed – the bed *he had been in* – and could text him again.

I asked him if this meant we were going out, boyfriend and girlfriend, and he said 'if you want' so nonchalantly I decided not to mention it again. In a way this felt even more exciting, even more adult. To not only be making out with someone – to have been naked with someone – but to not even be dating them, to have something so special and unique and wonderful that boring labels like that didn't even matter –

He asked me to shave *down there*, something I'd never thought about doing, didn't know where to begin. Were there special razors, did you have to use a cream? I didn't shave at all, my underarm hair was soft but getting longer, my legs were downy, but I said of course I would, sure, if that's what he wanted.

Then, after about a week of this, he stopped texting me back.

xix.ii

I thought about the cuts on his arm and the way he had cried going down on me and I thought maybe he was dead. I thought if he had killed himself that it was my fault. I had said the wrong thing, or failed to say the right one. I had made it all about my desire for him, my body, my nervousness, I had not given him whatever space in me he had come to find –

But then I saw him posting on Facebook, and I became an expert in tracking someone's life from a distance. Or, at least, the fact of their living. He was alive; he just did not want me.

Camp Three: The 22nd World Scout Jamboree, Sweden

Tonight the super trouper beams are gonna blind me/ But I won't feel blue / Like I always do / 'Cause somewhere in the crowd there's you (ABBA, 'Super Trouper')

xx.i

THE World Scout Jamboree takes place every four years somewhere in the world. In 2011 it was in Sweden.

I had undergone a fairly rigorous – to my eyes, at least – selection process; a written application, then a training weekend complete with interview. Thrown together with strangers, I had quickly attached myself to two people (neither of whom eventually got selected) and embraced the experience. Now, I remember very little about it, other than the shock of suddenly living in close quarters with people I'd never met before. It was like being doused in cold water. By the end of the first night, having struggled to put up our tents, my new friends and I were linking arms and confiding secrets. Underneath it all, though, was a new tenseness: we all wanted to get selected, to spend the next year fundraising and having training camps, to get to go to Sweden.

Over the course of the year, we had four long weekend

camps away to get to know each other. Essex was sending three Units, of 28 Scouts and Guides each. Each Unit was ascribed a bright neon colour and an ABBA song; we were the Super Troupers, clothed in a deep, bright pink that was visible for miles.

The Jamboree was the most exciting thing I'd ever been selected for. The idea was that Scouts from more wealthy countries would fundraise more, to pay the way for those from poorer countries, which made sense to me; the idea that it might not work out that way given the inequalities *within* a country didn't really occur to me. I got a weekly babysitting job, looked after my parents' friends' pets, ran an ABBA themed quiz at my school, packed bags... a friend of mine from the 26th, Kyle, and someone I'd known at Primary School from the 17th were also going, so the three of us often grouped together to raise money. (One evening we drove through the snow to Waitrose to pack bags; within half an hour of being inside, however, it became obvious that we'd made a huge mistake in failing to properly assess the weather and a storm was on its way. The car gave up on our way back and the three of us, unsuitably dressed in our scout uniforms, had to push it up a hill to get it working again. Snow falling, my shirt uncomfortably wet, laughing all the way.)

Over 40,000 Scouts attended the 22nd World Scout Jamboree in Rinkaby, Sweden, the opening ceremony of which took place on the 27th July 2011 and the closing one on the 6th August. I was one of those Scouts; so was James, my boyfriend. And so was Max.

xx.ii

I knew before flying, of course, that Max would be there. He'd told me the summer before; we'd joked about how we would exchange one campsite for another, a summer love affair on loop. He'd finally replied to one of my increasingly desperate messages at Easter, light hearted, ignoring the frantic texts I'd been sending for almost a year. He said of course he still had my necklace and he hoped he'd see me on the Jamboree. That was it – nothing to say he missed me, he loved me, that last summer had meant anything to him even approaching what it had to me. But it was enough of a lifeline.

Before reaching Sweden, the whole UK contingent flew to Copenhagen. That was the best chance I would have to find him, I thought: there'd only be around 3,000 Scouts in one fairly small city, split between several hostels, but all meeting at the Tivoli Gardens theme park the first evening and for a big UK contingent party on the second. (Alphabeat performed.) So the chances of running into him there weren't *huge*... but they weren't tiny, either.

xxi

IN 1920, an alternative to Baden-Powell's scouting movement was set up by John Hargrave, who had recently been overlooked as the Gilwell camp chief. (Gilwell Park Camp remains one of the headquarters of Scouting in Britain, especially for leadership training.). Called the Kindred of the Kibbo Kift – a name which, as Matthew De Abaitua points out, seems 'to be drawn directly from the Ku Klux Klan' – Hargrave's group divided their time between 'the writing of songs and poetry, the playing of music, embroidery of banners, the fashioning of puppets and masks, and trials to harden the spirit and stiffen the sinews'. Emotional and physical resilience and experience grew hand in hand. Thoreau, too, who plucked his meditation on living in the wilderness for two years out of nature and into a book, ends with the meditation that 'the earth is not a mere fragment of dead history, stratum upon stratum like the leaves of a book, to be studied by geologists and antiquaries chiefly, but living poetry like the leaves of a tree, which precede flowers and fruit'. *Walden* is one giant, misogynistic, patchwork attempt at turning living outside in a poem.

It wasn't poetry that sums up the flight to Denmark for me, though, but music. Specifically, the song 'A Lack of

Understanding' by The Vaccines. (It *was* 2011). For those readers who might not be *au fait* with the early 2010s indie music scene, the song starts off like this:

> It's only been a year
> But it feels like a lifetime here.
> How's it been for you?
> Does it feel like a lifetime too?

iPod in my ears, sitting next to the boyfriend I had promised to sleep with but knew with a sick certainty I never would, I set the song to repeat. How could it have been a whole year since last summer? A lifetime indeed: a year in which I'd gotten accepted into a prestigious boy's grammar school for sixth form; dated someone for eight months, despite my residual crush on Lucy and my monstrous love for Max; started working a Saturday job in the fried chicken shop at the local zoo; started a bewildering friendship with a 23-year-old man who had recently graduated, who had approached me looking at the science fiction section of a bookshop.

That man and I spent long hours on the phone to each other discussing the various merits of that week's *Doctor Who* and the tantalising possibilities of Amy Pond, or talking about what we'd been reading; I was flattered by his attention and interest, and took pleasure in making my boyfriend jealous by pretending to flirt back with him. He'd confessed his love for me a few months back and I hadn't thought much of it. I was used to boys falling in love with me: Ben, James, what was one more friend whose feelings I didn't think I'd ever be capable of reciprocating? The fact that he was seven years older than me didn't seem to matter, even when he got explicit, even when he got nasty. The idea of *grooming* had never crossed my mind. But James and I had recently had another argument about him and my refusal to stop being friends with him, so the topic of other boys as we boarded the plane was a touchy one. I had told him only in passing about Max, skirting around the reality of the topic; the reality of who I knew, without any tendril-doubt, would be waiting for me. The only question was when.

xxii.i

FIRST night in a new city, abroad without your parents, freedom that feels like adulthood. I wasn't with James. Why didn't we sneak off to a hostel room, his or mine? I'd made up some excuse; instead, that first evening, I was in Tivoli Gardens with a friend called Greg. I don't know why we'd split up from everyone else, why we weren't in a huge group with the rest of our friends, I don't know how much of it I was planning, but I know I was eyeing up every group we came across to see where in the UK they came from, searching for Sussex, I know that my attention was distracted and my mind skitterish. If I could just find him –

Then, suddenly, he was there.

It sounds fake, I know, but I met him again the first night, just as I knew I would. We made eye contact and then we were kissing, like nothing had happened, like I wasn't with someone who knew my boyfriend, like all of Max's friends weren't there staring at the two of us, Rollercoasters and the excitement of thousands of Scouts as the backdrop to a magical, fateful reunion. How could it not be meant to be? How could *we* not be meant to be? He was wearing my necklace! How could that not be a sign?

I knew I'd find you, he said.

THE assonance of writing this then going on Facebook only to be reminded that it was nine years to the day The hot Danish night. Chatting to Scouts from Australia in the queue for a rollercoaster ride who were shocked wide awake with their jetlag. Not telling anyone how my heart was racing every time I saw someone who might have been him. And how, when it finally was, I found myself perfectly calm.

Why is it that someone can hurt you so much in so many ways and you will still, many years later, now happily and wildly and nicely in love, want to reach out to them and say *hey do you remember –* ?

Early on in this project I skyped James. We talked about Scouts and our memories of the Jamboree. I wanted to ask him about that night, me cheating on him, the way the Jamboree collapsed around Max for me. I wanted to ask what he remembered, how he felt. But in the end I was too embarrassed – how do you say to an old friend, *hey, did you know that night that I'd cheated on you? Or was it later?* How do you ask, *did I look changed when I came back to the hostel? Could you see that I was burstinghappy for the first time in a year? I felt like I was shining.*

So neither of us mentioned it, and I have no-one else I can

ask.

Please understand: this memory is like a prized piece of fruit. I've spent so many years hiding it away, greedily, and now finally I can smash it open. So peer at the pulp, tell me I was wrong. Tell me it meant nothing, that it was a coincidence. That I misunderstood his presence there, his wearing my necklace, as more than it was. Tell me there is no such thing as fate. Tell me it's okay, finally, to throw it away.

xxiii

I don't know how to tell this right. It's a self-justification, really: if you only understood, you could not possibly judge me for what I did or didn't do later.

Why do I care so much about someone I don't know judging me?

xxiv.i

I returned to the hostel fizzing with joy. Max and I had kissed, we had talked. He had given me a carefully printed out card with his phone number on; we were encouraged to make these before leaving to have to hand for all the stranger-friends you would make on camp. Name, photo, email address: the aim was to return with a bunch of these to your respective connections, to send out Facebook invitations, to hold onto the feeling of the Jamboree for a little bit longer. Max's was green cardboard, unlaminated, with a photo of him in a stupid hat smirking at the camera. I couldn't stop touching it.

When I eventually realised I had to leave, Greg had gone. Overwhelmed with panic that I wouldn't be able to find my way back, Max walked with me around the park until I caught a glimpse of a familiar neon pink. The friends I ran into looked at me suspiciously as I gestured at Max, gabbled about running into a friend from another Unit, about losing Greg accidently (*please God let him not have already told anyone let this knowledge not have seeped out*), about not knowing the way back to the hostel. I left Max with a slightly-too-long hug and walked away with his promise that we'd seek each other out in Sweden, that now we had found one another again nothing could get in the way.

This wasn't true, obviously. Several things could. One of those things was waiting for me in the lobby, playing cards.

RIGHT now, I want to text my boyfriend with a plea. *Don't ever stop loving me.* You can't demand these things of people – I know that, now. You can't promise you won't change. You can only promise that right now, you don't want to, that you don't want to envisage a future where you're not together. That present desire for the future always has to be enough. I know that.

With Max, I never had a present, which is why it felt so temporally *fucked.* It was always delayed: I loved him in the promise of a future tense. That evening, I felt sick when I saw James sitting with his friends, waiting for me. He kept trying to talk to me and I would mumble and shut him down. I was nervously playing with Max's card, obsessively. He asked me to come outside with him and said, 'so... did you find your friend?' I said yes. He didn't ask anything more: didn't say, *did you kiss him,* didn't say *do you still love him.* We kissed goodnight and that was the last time we kissed on that trip. In the end, I couldn't tell him. I was too – I was so happy.

We all do things as teenagers we're ashamed of as adults, right? Isn't that the point? A lot of my friends cheated on their boyfriends or were cheated on. We kissed each other at parties and in parks and pretended nothing had happened the next day at school. I don't want to undermine the cruelty of that, but I also don't think it was always a big deal: it wasn't always traumatic. Most of those relationships were based on mutual attraction and having a laugh; I'm impressed by couples who have been together since school because I think, *wow, you actually liked each other?* Imagine having the foresight to know what you wanted at that age.

This isn't – I don't want to make excuses. It was as wrong then as now; there's never any excuse for cheating on someone. I had kissed a girl at a party a few months before, and James hadn't seemed bothered, which wasn't – it wasn't a reason. I knew he'd be upset. But I couldn't think of it as wrong to kiss Max, not really. Not when it was so obviously the properly romantic thing to do. I loved him, didn't I? I'd loved him for a year. And he loved me. He was wearing my fucking *necklace*. So kissing him was the right thing to do, the Disney thing to do, the storybook thing to do. The *only* thing to do. Nothing in me could properly regret it.

The next day the smoke still hadn't cleared. We spent the day in Copenhagen; everywhere I went my skin was on edge, but this time, no such luck. And I avoided James for the most part – avoided the conversation that couldn't not be coming – until, eventually, it was time for the UK contingent's party.

3,000 Scouts. A band playing pop songs we all knew. The

absolute excitement in the air, thick at the back of your throat, because we would be driving to the Jamboree site *tomorrow*. We were given vouchers for free food and queued up, the second night in a row, for burgers and chips. The sun was out.

I don't remember what I wore. What excuse I made to my friends. When exactly I peeled myself away from them looking for Max. But again, I was driven by the absolutely certainty of finding him: the inevitability of our love.

I found him outside, eventually – the stage was set up in a big tent, but there was a big outside court too – with his friends, the same ones from the night before. He was wearing eyeliner and cat ears, like a girl on halloween, and we spent the rest of the night together. Kissing in front of everyone – no, *making out*, the way you can only do in public when it's your first love – holding hands, dancing, not caring who saw us.

xxiv.iii

OF course, everyone saw me. Us. Everyone saw us.

XXV

WE drove to Sweden the next day. James refused to look at me; none of his friends would either. I never found out exactly what happened – if he saw us himself, or if someone else did and told him. I was too ashamed to find out.

Or... no. Actually, no. I just didn't *care*. All I could think about was finding Max when we finally got to the Jamboree campsite.

We drove across the Øresund bridge from Copenhagen to Malmø before driving to the campsite. The bus was hot but everyone was in a good mood – James and I aside, of course. I sat next to Caz, chattering with excitement, and by some horrible accident of fate James and Morgan ended up on the seats in front of us. The shared effort of avoiding eye contact could have powered the whole thing. When we got to the campsite we had to carry our heavy bags for about an hour in the heat; it must have felt like we'd never reach our spot. We did, of course. We put up the specially designed Jamboree tents, and constructed the wooden gateway we'd prepared; we unpacked our belongings and were issued with our ID cards and neckers. We learnt the layout of the Summer subcamp: the shop where we could get fresh food every day (we took turns cooking); the toilets, of course, and showers; the paths to the main square, where all our activities would take place; the internet tent where we could queue up for computer access; the noticeboard where important international news would be posted...

My Jamboree unit, and home camp. The sun was resolutely not shining when this photo was taken.

We also met our neighbours. Two pitches down was another UK group, this one from Durham. Next door was a French Unit. To our other sides, a Brazilian Unit and a Russian one. One evening we were tasked with either cooking dinner for or attending another Unit's site for dinner, a sort of international *Come Dine With Me*. My patrol went to the Brazilians' for dinner. Everyone was friendly – I felt ashamed that English was the automatic common language, but grateful too, and ended up giggling together with two Russian girls like we'd been friends for years. They cooked some sort of rice thing, I think – there was a lot of rice on camp. Carbs are easy icebreakers.

The reason I mention the Durham camp is because that first night or second, I hooked up with a boy there. Daniel. This might destroy the image of myself as a romance-struck waif, but it feels important to be honest. It was mostly retaliation for James' apparent lack of any upset at my actions. He'd already started up a new relationship – or very intense friendship, at least – with another girl in our Unit. I was furious, demonising her behind her back at every opportunity, firing cruel insults about her personal appearance. It stung, the fact that James must have been interested in her before ever we broke up, and getting with a stranger rubbed it in his face: *I can do this now. You don't care? I care even less than you.*

It was a mistake, of course. Daniel clung to me like a limpet for the rest of the camp, until I was making excuses not to walk past his pitch, to go the long way to the toilets so I could avoid seeing him. That first night he flirted awkwardly, his palm clammy in my hand, as we walked together to the first big event of the Jamboree: the opening ceremony.

xxvi.i

THE weather wasn't great for the opening ceremony. It was windy – Bear Grylls, who was doing the official handover as Chief Scout of Great Britain, had to abseil onto the stage instead of paragliding – and it sprinkled with rain. But the thrill in the air! 40,000 people who'd been waiting at least a year for this moment. The official Jamboree song, 'Changing the World' which we'd all listened to prior to leaving, was performed. Listening back to it in order to write this, I was stunned to realise that it still brings me almost to tears. The lyrics are lodged somewhere in my brain along with all the other pop songs of being a teenager. The words that seemed so loaded with meaning it was amazing anyone could listen casually.

There was a flag from every country, carried by a Scout, in the manner of all parades. I've carried the flag for my Troop or Unit before at various events – St George's Day, Remembrance Day – and it's difficult to describe how it makes you feel. For one thing, it's heavy. I can't have been the only one tormented with an idea of loosening my grip accidentally and ending up knocking people out with the flag pole, centre of entirely the wrong sort of attention. But then, the physical effort and anxiety aside, comes the pride. It's hypnotic, you know, and I could always see suddenly why Americans invested so much worth and importance into theirs. One in every classroom – yes, of course. The embodiment of what we all want, at least sometimes: to belong. To be a part of something.

Of course, the US flag excludes as much as it includes. All of them do. But for this opening ceremony that was at least as much of a joy as belonging: seeing almost all the countries in the world represented in one place, feeling part of something truly international. For the rest of the camp they'd be lined up along the main path, so you would walk by them all on the way to and from various activities – or whilst exploring – and remember where you were, how real it all was.

xxvi.ii

THE actual body of the Jamboree camp was, much like any other, divided into structured activities. Of course, all the adults involved recommended we kept a detailed daily diary, and of course none of us did – at least, I didn't, convinced I'd remember everything. Just as predictably, the activities themselves have faded beyond any real clarity, leaving me with nothing but disconnected memories (and, luckily, a lot of photos):

1. Caz, my best friend on camp, flirting with a group of American Boy Scouts we met at an activity which included planning a city for the future. In a photo I took, she's hiding behind a frisbee with one of them, who she'd later have her first kiss with; I still have him on Facebook. He's a professional musician now. We played frisbee with them after dinner on several evenings and one of them gave me a baseball hat from a campsite I will probably never go to.

2. Almost burning down the entire campsite when my frying pan burst into flames and I instinctively swung it off the heat and into the bunting we'd

put up around the site's edges. Our patrol had decided that for the meal we were in charge of, we weren't going to do rice or pasta, but instead make chips for everyone; it took hours (and more frying than I ever wish to undertake again) but let me tell you, we were popular that evening.

3. My patrol sneaking off to sit in hammocks in the woods on one of the hottest days, braiding bracelets, lying on each other's stomachs, staring up into the trees.

4. Wandering over to the food table, and eating whatever could be easily thrown together; there was a brief Unit-wide craze for bananas dipped in chocolate spread. The stock of the shop changed daily, and it was always a guessing game to purchase and carry home enough food for all 40 of us. I don't think we ever got it *wrong* – there was always something to eat – but that might not always end up being an assortment of food that looked like a meal.

5. Every unit went off-site for something called, grandly, *Camp in Camp*. Some spent theirs camped out overnight, by the sea, maybe. Ours spent all day offsite in separate patrols, hiking, accompanied by a patrol of Swedish scouts. It

was a beautifully clear hot day and it finally felt like we were getting to see some of the country. The hike was mostly flat, green trees and brooks. We refilled our bright yellow Jamboree branded water bottles with spring water straight from the source. Everything you drank from them tasted metallic, and I was scared of being poisoned, but in the end thirst won out, and the water was far from stagnant – it was crisp, and fresh, and delicious. We had a picnic and posed for a group photo. Fred's bottle imploded on itself, the heat and metal suction having created a vacuum. Caz and I walked with Warwick, who's engaged now, and he took a photo of me, American cap on, sunglasses, tanned skin, beaming. Having walked for miles, we ended up at an ice cream shop, where we thankfully shrugged off our rucksacks and sprawled over each other with reckless exhaustion. Our patrol leader, one of the oldest of us – he was almost eighteen – fell asleep on the coach on the way back. We got back to the main site in the evening. Glowing.

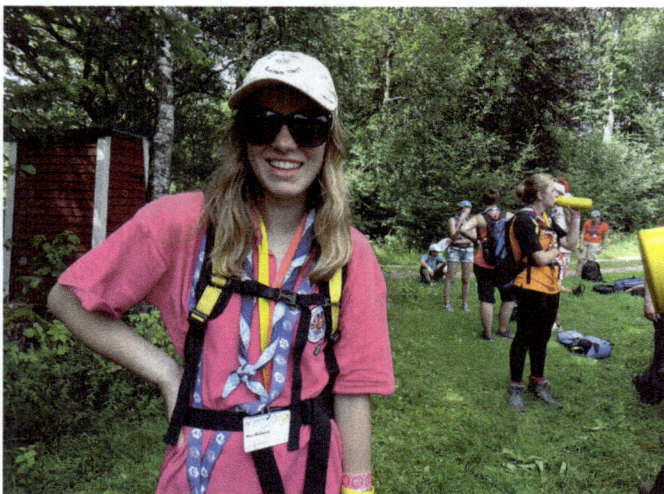

Camp on Camp: taking a break from hiking.

6. There was a viewing tower that you could climb up to see the whole site spread out in front of you like toys. I went up with Daniel, unable to think of an excuse not to (or perhaps simply not sick of him yet) – the only photo that I have from the tower shows the two of us smiling awkwardly, his arm around me, the Sylvanian-family like tiny cuteness of the campsite behind us. I regret not going alone. I look sad, I think, and I know it's because I was scanning the ground for Max, wishing it was him with his arm around me and a proud grin. It should be a lovely photo.

7.   The world culture fair, a day when everyone dressed up, made food, put on performances to represent their home countries. We'd practised multiple different recipes on one of our training camps before settling on steamed puddings – not too difficult to make on a campsite, was the theory – and they were just about edible. I ate more salted liquorice than I should admit to whilst chatting with a Swedish boy named Momo; my friend Jack, who went on to study languages, spent so much time helping our French neighbours make crepes that we declared him "Jacques" and a traitor. Cardboard signs bloomed all over the site: 'Turn, bitches! Belgium!' reads one I took photograph of; 'We invented Harry Potter, U jelly?' proclaims another, setting it in time like nothing else. We wandered around learning dances and card games, seeing instruments we couldn't even name let alone play, talking to everyone.

I don't think I can emphasise enough just how social the campsite was. It wasn't unusual to go to the toilet and take two hours because on your way back, you'd met a group of Scouts from Brazil, say, who were sitting around playing a guitar and shouting at you to come and sit with them. Everyone was interested in each other; a lot of the time, we exchanged email addresses and contact details, but it was just as likely we'd never speak again. The energy of the site was built on these precipitous chance encounters, fleeting engagements with people just as delighted to be there as you were. The world culture day epitomised that. There are videos of it online – I strongly suggest you look them up – just because of the joy that seeps out. We really were that happy. It's not an act. The whole campsite felt – good. A good, friendly place to be. But the best thing about the world culture fair, for me, was our play.

xxvi.iii

WE had been told, months in advance, that we would be required to have a *performance* which accurately represented our culture. It was made – as so many things in Scouting are – to seem much more formal than it turned out to be. Several ideas had been rejected as requiring too much equipment or co-ordination, and eventually we'd come up with the idea of running a sort of combined fashion show and sketch show. Each pair of 'actors' would be dressed as something representing English culture. They would walk on 'stage' and act according to their roles: we had a 'cop and robber' chasing each other to the Hoosiers, Romeo proposing to Juliet with Taylor Swift playing in the background, George slaying the dragon, Doctor Who... it finished off with the Queen waving to everyone, of course (I think the song for that might have been 'Fat Bottomed Girls', a joke funny to almost nobody but me). I was somehow in charge of directing this whole thing – possibly only because I owned the required pair of battery powered iPod speakers – and I did my absolute best.

We'd practiced it at the last training camp which had taken place in the final run up to GCSE exams. Caz would sit next to me earnestly controlling the music, the 'actors' made up their short sequences, and the whole thing had begun to clumsily slot into place. We'd grandly called it a showcase, put out requests for costumes, and made room in our precious luggage allowance for the things we'd need... and finally it was time. I hounded everyone together and we got dressed as proudly and nervously as if we were going to perform to the whole camp. All morning, wandering around the world culture fair and making friends, we'd been inviting people to our performances, but one of the problems with a camp like that was how little connection to time you had. What does 3pm mean in a day that hangs limp with possibility?

So, in the end, fewer people then we'd anticipated in our nerves came to view the showcase. But some did, and – I am still proud of this – they enjoyed it. We'd created something genuinely *funny*, in a day when it felt like so much was on offer: food, and games, and performances, beautiful clothes and everyone bubbling over with the chance to show off. We'd made some sort of mark, and for years I had the group photo as my laptop background like a monument, a crystallised moment of happiness.

There's a clue in the photo, though, that not everything was going smoothly to plan, although it's a clue which nobody but me and my leaders (and those people I confided in) could ever have picked up on. Once again, I had found myself in trouble with the adults who stood in for my parents; once again I found a camp united in scandal against me, an unfair whisper network of mingled awe, surprise, and resentment.

Once again, of course, it was all Max's fault.

My showcase cast, triumphant post-performance.

W H E N we'd said goodbye in Copenhagen, the only way I had to locate Max was the name of his subcamp. Since there were only four – they were divided into the seasons – this didn't feel like a lot to go on, but I was buoyed up by the success I'd had at Tivoli, I felt compelled by fate. James had been ignoring me more or less entirely – and I later found out that the leaders had come across him crying one evening and comforted him, so any coldness I felt from them might not have been entirely imagined – but we'd more or less brushed over any serious scandal. People still liked me, and the experience of the Jamboree was all consuming, pushing any thoughts about other people's relationships away. Besides, most people were preoccupied with flirtations of their own: James and his new girlfriend were only one of the couples to form, despite the very serious talks we'd had on sex and being sensible on site.

They'd been pretty stringent about it on the training camps. On one weekend – ironically at Thriftwood – we'd been staying in cabins indoors, two bunkbeds to a room. It was January. We had a late Christmas party; I had a dark pink stripe in my hair and wore a denim shirt despite the cold. I remember that

I had been nervous about the location. Thriftwood already felt haunted to me: the ghost of that summer, of Max and I by the lake. I probably texted him: *guess where I'm spending the weekend?* hoping that the memories would prove as intoxicating for him as they were for me, though I should have known by then that that wasn't the case.

Anyway, James and I went to bed on time, and then snuck out, prearranged, to go for a walk in the woods and make out against a tree. History repeats itself: we lost track of time, one of the leaders did a surprise check on the rooms, my bed was empty, his was too, they put two and two easily together. When we returned it was to a row of glaring adults. By now, I was accustomed to this: he was a bit more embarrassed. I returned to my room where my friends giggled and teased me, and I pretended everything was fine. That was the first time I realised exactly how bad experiences have a habit of forcing themselves back upon you. How easy it is to make mistakes and fall into a pattern. *I have done this before,* your body thinks, slipping back into train-track routes, reinforcing them. Maybe I thought that next time would be different. Maybe I thought that if I proved I was the same person, wherever he was Max would somehow know, somehow still want me.

In Sweden, then, I went looking for him in the daytime. We had plenty of free time to explore, to make friends, play cards – scheduled activities were mostly in the morning or afternoon and four or five hours at most. I dragged Greg along with me, the same friend I'd been with in Tivoli, a magical-thinking spell, like if I could replicate enough of the circumstances the clouds would part and Max would appear. I can't remember if I told him the truth behind our trip or not – if I didn't, I doubt he was fooled. We went to the subcamp Max had specified and I started looking for any UK Units, though the pitches were mostly empty and it felt like the chances of finding him were slight.

Then – and I swear, I'm not making this up – I found his site. It seemed empty but I saw the banner. And just when I was thinking to myself, okay, I know where he is now, I can come back at dinner or something, he stepped out of a tent in front of me.

Except he wasn't alone.

xxviii.i

I hoard these memories like pearls, shells, shattered glass rendered numb by the waves:

- that she was called Hannah
- that she was welsh
- that she had dark hair and stood too close to him and they came out of his tent where they'd surely been fucking
- that Greg made an excuse to leave and I made myself act like everything was fine
- that he was still wearing my damn necklace
- that he looked at me like he loved me

I told him where my pitch was, acting like it was just a coincidence I was there at all. I pretended I had to get back for something, that I had no time for him, that it was lovely to meet her, that I didn't care about what they'd been doing. That it was none of my business.

Maybe it was none of my business. Maybe I'd been stupid to think that what had passed between us, first in Thriftwood and in Colchester, then a year later in Denmark, meant anything. I told myself I wouldn't go and find him again; if he wanted to see me, he knew where I was. I left hoping. I left embarrassed. I left wishing it had been me he'd taken into his tent in the middle of the day.

xxviii.ii

IN series six of *Buffy the Vampire Slayer*, Buffy starts what is usually referred to as a 'turbulent' sexual relationship with the 'neutered' vampire Spike. Originally one of the show's arch villains, Spike becomes a reluctant force for good when a chip implanted in his head prevents him from harming humans. He insists that he is *still evil*, just physically prevented from acting on it. But then he falls in love with Buffy.

At first she is disgusted. At the end of series five, she dies. 'The hardest thing in this world is to live in it', she tells her sister Dawn, before sacrificing herself. When her friends bring her back to life, with dark magic and love, she cannot bring herself to tell them why she is so depressed: that she was not in a hell dimension as they thought, but in heaven. In comparison to heaven this world is "hard and bright and violent"; it is too much, all too much, all the time, why won't they *leave her alone*, why do they expect her to be happy, why do they expect her to care –

Spike and Buffy don't sleep together until he finds out that he can hurt her. "You came back *wrong*", he sneers. She latches onto it: a reason for her depression, a reason for her desire for Spike. They fight and then they fuck. A house crumbles all around them. You get it, right. It's a metaphor.

Spike loves Buffy, and she is depressed, so occasionally she makes him tell her: "tell me that you love me. Tell me that you want me." "I love you. I want you."

When, eventually, Buffy realises she is hurting Spike – and using him to hurt herself – she breaks up with him. In an attempt to get her back, to make her realise that what he feels is real and what they have is good, Spike tries to rape her.

It's a shocking scene, for many reasons, and it's the cause of fandom controversy almost twenty years on. I hate the raped woman trope. I find it uncomfortable to watch, and I hate the way the camera shows Spike's slow realisation of what he's done, the way horror blossoms like a bruise across his face. I want it to be easy: he's in the wrong. I don't want to be forced to feel sorry for him.

But the real reason it's shocking is because it undoes the narrative fans wanted and had come to expect. Despite Spike's insistence that he was still evil, series five and six show him becoming more and more involved with the main characters, part of the gang. This is intended to show that we were wrong, too, that like Buffy we had been misguided. That just because he says he *loves* her didn't mean it was good and romantic. This is sex as self-harm, self-loathing, pain; this is sex as a way of feeling something in a world that you're numb to; this is love as a weapon. This is bad sex that is not redeemable by love: it is not the plotline we want. It is uncomfortable and dangerous.

I wish I'd seen it as a teenager. We need more depictions of relationships that aren't black or white; that are *bad*. We need to have the conversation about what it looks like when love isn't good, when the house crumbles around you.

Max idolised Spike.

xxviii.iii

WHEN he came, he came barefoot. He'd walked across the entire Jamboree site like that. I commented on it and he looked down as if he hadn't realised. His feet were filthy.

He wasn't welcome at my site, unsurprisingly, so we walked back across to his. It was after dinner but still light: warm enough to both be wearing shorts. We got there and chatted to his friends, to each other. One of the guys, who I'd also met briefly in Tivoli – whose name I didn't know, and wish I had – took me aside to say that I deserved better. He knew about the other girl too; he said something like, *you don't have to settle for this.* I think I just shrugged: like I'd made my bed, like I had no agency in anything that happened. I was propelled by guilt and love. If I developed morals now, breaking up with James like I did would all have been for nothing; if I confronted Max about her and he didn't choose me, what would have been the point of any of it?

So maybe by this point I knew better than to hope Max would choose me, if I asked him to.

Anyway, I remember another thing he said: that he'd fallen in love with me last summer instantly. That he'd been

in love with me ever since. He said: *it's fate that we met again*
and then once more he was leading me towards a tent, his
friends egging him on, his leaders nowhere to be seen.

xxviii.iv

WE probably would have had sex. I don't know if I would have stopped him – which isn't to imply that I would have been unwilling, just that it wasn't the ideal situation in which to lose my virginity. I do know that we'd both stripped completely naked, that it was hot and dark in the tent, that night had set, when Max was called out. Their Unit was going on camp-in-camp the next day and he had a quick meeting; he promised me it wouldn't take long. I stayed there, on top of his sleeping bag, listening to the discussion as best I could. I'm not sure how long I was there for. My skin was tingling with nerves and anticipation.

The tent opened. It wasn't him. Two other boys tore it open, with a flash camera, and snapped a photo before I swore at them, scrabbling around for something to cover myself with. I don't know whether it was that or someone else saying something, but suddenly his leaders knew I was there – a woman was talking to me through the tent, telling me to get dressed and get out.

I couldn't find my underwear or my shorts. So I put his shorts on, with nothing underneath, and left. He walked me back some of the way apologising for what had happened, telling me we'd see each other again soon, kissing me goodbye. I slipped into my own tent and told Caz everything, joy spilling through every crack in me. That night, I slept in his shorts. It's those I'm wearing in the showcase photo, taken the next day. Touching them felt like touching him; like he was still against my skin.

UNBELIEVABLE

as it seems – and it was unbelievable then, becomes more so in the retelling, has never ceased to seem like myth or fable, like something with its own internal momentum, of romance, perhaps, or fate – the next day, too, repeated the year before.

After breakfast, I was coming back from the toilets with a friend when one of our leaders asked me to come over. I couldn't think – genuinely couldn't think – what it might be about. They seemed uncomfortable, shifty, and I was blandly happy, when suddenly they presented me with a supermarket carrier bag: *can you explain this to us*? I looked in. My shorts and underwear looked back.

Imagine, please, being sixteen and already out of your depth and four adults assuming you'd had sex and confronting you with the evidence. TJ giving me 'the talk' had been bad enough; this was excruciating. One of them asked me what I'd been doing – which, in retrospect, was not the best question in the world, as if it wasn't obvious – and I answered with something panic-flippant. "It was hot in there", I said. Digging myself the same hole I'd found myself occupying at Thriftwood, of unstable slut, sexually promiscuous dickhead who'd screw over her lovely boyfriend and make out with strangers from Durham and fuck the love of her life in a dirty tent, I added, numbly, "we didn't have sex". They told me that didn't matter; that his leaders had come over (how did they know where to go, I wondered) the night before and had a talk about Max, and me, and the two of us. Once more I wonder what they were told, how much they knew of him, how closely his leaders had looked at the crisscrossed scars on his arms.

At this stage, I was still fervently against the logic and kindness of my leaders, who were blindly overlooking all the other sneaking about that was going on onsite. I felt victimised. No one understand how all of this – finding him in Tivoli, finding him here, finding him at all – was a miracle. None of them had heard the way he told me he loved me, the way we'd talked as we walked across the site, about TV and school and what we'd done over the past year, about the music he'd been listening to and the musical theatre he'd seen and his hopes of studying performance or theatre or music at university. He could be so kind, so funny.

He didn't have to come to find me, did he? But he did; he walked barefoot and said that Hannah had meant nothing to him, not like me, the girl he'd loved for a year, the one who knew how sad he was, how his dad's death had corroded him like rust. It was sprinkled over everything he did. I think of him touching me now as if it left behind stains; as if it's always that first time, and we are lying together in my narrow single bed, and he is raising his head from between my legs and his eyes are dark with tears I wish I hadn't seen.

xxiv.i

THE Jamboree sparked out with a storm. Although we'd had showers, sometimes heavy, it only really *poured* the night of the closing ceremony. Of course we'd already packed away our belongings and tents – we were leaving early in the morning, 4am or so, and so we had to stay in our uniform all night and the next day – meaning we huddled under the main tent, bags and all, waiting until it began. Luckily we'd been equipped with some bizarre and unflattering waterproof jackets to wear over our shirts, but it very easily could have been miserable. Not to mention the end-feeling, the sense of things drawing to a close, the broken-hearted horror of saying goodbye to the space that had acted as our home for almost two weeks.

There were fireworks, speeches, and (inexplicably) the band Europe playing 'The Final Countdown': at every break in the storm, thousands of Scouts started cheering, sending up Mexican waves, waving at every video camera in view. The night seemed endless. Our Unit would be spending the next on the coach to Stockholm, then getting an overnight ferry to Helsinki for the next part of the trip – known as Home Hospitality (or HoHo), this was our chance to stay with local Scouts and their families. Dripping back in the rain at the end of the ceremony, we all curled up under the main tent, uncomfortable on our bags as we waited out the rest of the night. Tents magnify rain: even the thunder and lightning feels distant in comparison, when every drop is amplified on the thin sheet above you.

Even exhausted after the dancing, energetic joy of the closing ceremony, I didn't sleep. Max had told me he'd come to say goodbye. This was the last night we would ever be in walking distance of each other – surely he would come?

Dawn came, and we straggled onto the coach, and set off for Stockholm. Everyone was devastated to be leaving: I didn't have to excuse myself for crying, although I think maybe only James knew that there was more to what it was that I was crying for.

xxiv.ii

WHILST we had been onsite in Sweden, news had trickled in intermittently. Some people had bought their phones with them, but opportunities to charge things were rare and data was expensive. There was, if you could be bothered to queue, an internet cafe – ten or so computers in a tent. One day, Caz and I went there to log on, which I remember primarily because it turned out James had messaged my sister in a fit of anger and she'd diligently reported back: *is it true you broke up?* she asked from a large family holiday in the South of France.

The more reliable ways to get news was through the onsite newspapers which were distributed every few days with a report of global information, or through our leaders. It was the first of these – or maybe just word-of-mouth spreading across the campsite – that first told us what was going on back home. It was the summer of 2011: London had been hit by riots. We couldn't get much information, just vague reports of shop windows smashed in, buildings on fire, the whisper that a death had started it. This – the murder of Mark Duggan by Metropolitan police on the 4th August – was the official catalyst, but the riots spread beyond that. To not be in the country as this went on meant that it took on a weird, shadowy existence in our collective imagination: it seemed impossible to understand that London was on fire when we couldn't *see* it.

When we got to Finland we were separated: 9 of us, plus a leader, went to a small town in the East named Mikkelli. We had partnered with the local Scout Troop: Caz, Sarah and I were hosted by a Scout called Camilla and her parents. They lived in a flat with an upstairs neighbour who was a chef, and each mealtime was an absolute feast after two weeks of camping food. For breakfast we ate piirakkat, or Karelian pastries – savoury pastries filled with a rice mixture – slathered in butter, and served with cheeses and ham; we were introduced to freshly picked lingonberries and yoghurt; lunches included rye bread, of course, and afterwards there were cardamon buns and deep, dark coffee.

The first thing the three of us did was ask to use Camilla's computer. She let us log on, and pulled up a chair as we scrolled in shock through two weeks of news. On Facebook, Em popped up to tell me about her new boyfriend, and to hear about what happened with Max; my sister had uploaded photos of my family suntanned and relaxed; everyone was talking about the riots. A photo of East London came up, a blaze of fire, and Caz said, barely in a whisper: "that's my house in the background". Suddenly the Jamboree seemed very far away.

THEY *wake up early, and head to the dock, where the Mikkelli Scout Troop have their boat. It is a beautiful boat with the required sauna, and they are sailing on lake Saimaa. According to Wikipedia, Mikkelli covers an area of 3,229.57 square kilometres (1,246.94 sq mi) of which 424.7 km2 (164.0 so mi) is water.*

They sail all day, playing cards and board games, teaching each other songs, taking photos, just chatting. The lake seems never ending, another world unfolding. Forbidding pine trees line the horizon in every direction. Eventually, they arrive at a small island. There's no other sign of human life. Breathing feels different.

Some of their leaders get the sauna going on the boat whilst some head off to the island to start a fire. The Scouts – English and Finnish alike – take turns sitting naked in the sauna and then diving into the cool lake. The contrast between suffocating heat and gasping cold makes their skin glow, their limbs tingle. It feels so fucking, magically alive. They do this for maybe an hour as the sun sets: the water glimmering orange, then pink, then purple, enticingly delicious. The sauna makes sense in a way that it never does in a British context, and she catches her friend's eye as the two of them dive off the edge of the boat, the two of them gasping with something they might never have felt otherwise, and thinks: I will never be able to do this moment justice, ever. And I will be trying to do so for my entire life.

Eventually, the night draws in and they all make their way reluctantly on land, leaving behind something they will surely never be able to get back. There, they cook sausages and snobrød on the fire and take photos of each other by the water. Finally it is dark and they crawl into their sleeping bags in the narrow depths of the boat, and sleep three to a bunk. In the morning, when they wake up, the boat will already be travelling back.

Interlude: 1 May 2012

I first saw you as my benediction / I am sorry you became my addiction / My game, my cold affliction (Yuck, 'Suck')

xxvi.i

ONCE again I was returning from a camp in a turmoil of uncertainty. How was I to explain the Jamboree to anyone without reference to Max, whose presence I had felt heavy every day on camp? How was I to explain the way I missed the friends I'd lived with, cooked with, slept in a tent with, for the best part of three weeks? We'd got to know each other over the year before, late nights talking on weekends away and training camps across Essex, dating each other and texting each other and making connections, but that had all been leading up to something. Now even those friendships felt dissolved, unsteady. We could meet up – there was the Essex Jamboree next summer – but we would never again all be in the same place, and we knew it. When a group like that ends, you miss the people you don't like or know well enough to keep in touch with of your own accord the most. I was sad not because of leaving my good friends, although the loss of Caz – who had shared my hostel in Copenhagen, my tent in Sweden and my room in Finland – especially hurt, but for the people I no longer had any real reason to talk to. And I finally had to face up to the end of my relationship; to tell my friends, to throw away the things he gave me, to do all the things you do when you disentangle your life from someone else's.

James hadn't said a word to me since the day we had taken a walk round the Jamboree site, ostensibly for me to answer his questions, although in reality I had just cried with my inability to explain what had felt so right to me but caused him so much pain. He asked me to take him to Max's campsite, which I had done unwillingly: when we got there, Max was busy shaving his initials into his leg hair, disarming James with both his femininity and his apparent welcome. Max had deflected his anger, and the three of us had parted ways uncertainly – Max looking at me with amused confusion, like, *why did you bring him here? hasn't he moved on by now? haven't you?* – but afterwards I had gone to meet some friends on the French campsite and found myself finally crying, embarrassingly heavy tears. Maybe it says something about me that it was the guilt which made me cry rather than the act of hurting James in the first place. I'd known all along that I'd done it, that I'd very publicly cheated on him, but actually witnessing his emotions was too much. I didn't know how to incorporate that into the narrative of my love story with Max. Just as I'd refused to face the reality of his tryst with Hannah, I refused to acknowledge, really, that I'd done wrong. It didn't *feel* wrong. Not like *not* kissing Max would have felt. The whole world and the importance of romance was on my side, mine and Max's, everything that had led to the two of us standing in a theme park at last, but James' hurt and anger needled at me uncomfortably. In the end, despite my anger and the way I bitched about her to my friends, I was almost glad when he found another girlfriend, just to absolve my guilt.

Well, whatever. It was all over now. My dad picked me up from the airport and I cried silently most of the way home, unsure what to do with the grief of leaving, unsure what these tears were even for. On the way home, I turned on my precious BlackBerry which I had carefully turned off and slipped into the glove compartment three weeks before, and anxiously scrolled through my texts and Facebook messages. Would his name pop up? Or had it really ended that last night in Sweden when he'd failed to turn up at my tent to say goodbye?

xxvi.ii

I had a day at home before I was back at my inglorious zoo-based fried chicken summer job and Holly and Em came round to see me. My mum opened the door to them and Em ran up the stairs and hurled herself into me: *I missed you* she said arms around me and I thought, o*h I guess we're this level of friends now*. And then I thought, *god, no, I missed you too.*

Em was, initially, a friend of my friend Sophie's. She'd started coming to Scouts occasionally, then joined Explorers with us when we moved up. At around the same time she had also moved to living down the road from me, so the three of us walked to school together. Em would walk the five minutes to mine and then the two of us would walk the five minutes to Sophie's: a carefully scheduled dance. The first conversation I remember the two of us having without Sophie to act as interlude was about the children's TV show *Rastamouse*, when she explained why she'd been late to mine. She asked if I watched it. I said no but, bemused by her enthusiasm, followed up with a promise that I would. By the end of the year she could have asked me to watch anything.

In the opposite way to how clearly I can pinpoint the

moment when Ellie and Holly and I started to become friends, the origins of my friendship with Em are shrouded in mystery. Some people you know right away are going to be important; others take time. Despite the fact that it was her I'd confessed to over Facebook whilst in Finland, detailing all the drama that had unfurled with James and Max, it still shocked me when she said she'd missed me. But by the end of that summer we were, silently but inextricably, linked together. Despite the fact we now went to different schools – I moved in order to attend the boys' Grammar which, controversially, accepted girls' into the sixth form – we now spent the majority of evenings together.

Every week the two of us would be driven to Explorers. By then, Sophie had more or less stopped coming. Most people had more or less stopped coming: some evenings there were only six or seven of us. Em, Holly, Ellie and I were sad about it – the Unit meant so much to us, had brought us together – but equally, although none of us would have said it, it had become so inherently *ours* that other people might have spoiled it. By then no-one else mattered.

Em would come round to mine after dinner for a chat and the two of us would end up falling asleep on my parents sofa fully clothed. I spent most of that year not changing for bed: I lived in black skinny jeans and a Beatles sweater. Part of this was depression, but part of it was how much time

173

the two of us spent together. We would lie on the same sofa to rewatch old episodes of *Doctor Who* and she would fall asleep on my legs. When I woke up in the morning she'd have quietly let herself out to go and do her paper round. We would lie on my bed listening to each other's identical, huge silver iPod classics: Bruce Springsteen, Joan Baez and Bob Dylan on hers; The Wonder Years, The Carpenters, and Wild Beasts on mine; Simon & Garfunkel, Taylor Swift and The Smiths on both. We listened to 'Cecilia' on an old vinyl, obsessively – *you're breaking my heart. You're shaking my confidence, baby.* At night we walked around the park, or we lay together on my bed sipping vodka from a bottle and playing the dictionary game, or we sat in the late-opening Costa attached to the cinema in town, bought large cups of coffee and talked about what books we were reading. We read *Brideshead Revisited* and loved it, then *A Handful of Dust*, so cruel and bittersweet Em cried, then *Scoop*. She borrowed my copy of *Tess of the D'Urbervilles* and I lent her Isabel Allende's *House of the Spirits*. She was studying *Frankenstein* and I read it in one sitting one night, so that I would understand what she was talking about. We read T.S. Eliot and Sylvia Plath together and wrote each other letters, long elaborate letters that I later dramatically burnt on a campfire, copying out pieces of prose or poems that had caught our hearts, or even that we'd written. I still remember reading Philip Larkin's 'Home is so sad' for the first time, copied out in Em's meticulous handwriting:

> Home is so sad. It stays as it was left,
> Shaped to the comfort of the last to go
> As if to win them back. Instead, bereft
> Of anyone to please, it withers so,
> Having no heart to put aside the theft
>
> And turn again to what it started as,
> A joyous shot at how things ought to be,
> Long fallen wide. You can see how it was:
> Look at the pictures and the cutlery.
> The music in the piano stool. That vase.

She wrote a long poem about a selkie and, embarrassed, lied and said she'd found it on the internet. I wrote bad *Waste Land* pastiche poems about our midnight walks: 'It is new to me, the idea that the concrete / could be kind'. We spun a world of words and heady teenage obsessions together like we were the first to do so, like everything was new. And every week we went to Scouts.

xxvi.iii

WHEN it was warm enough to do so we walked to the hut or walked back. Sometimes we went with Ellie, but more often it was just the two of us. Sometimes we went to Holly's first for dinner, to plan the evening's activities if it was one of us in charge. This was the Unit's greatest invention: the idea that the burden of planning a full programme of events would be put on us. We usually partnered up and did our best, drawing on any skills or knowledge we had that might be gainfully employed in entertaining (at most) twenty or so teenagers for two hours. Some ones that stick out:

1. Em's Roman evening, where we spent at least some of the time making mosaics out of magazines and spending far more energy on it than was perhaps sensible. I have a photo of her – or had, I don't know if it's been lost in the ether – delighted with herself, holding up a carefully crafted mosaic of a duck with such pride.

2. Fleur's ballet evening, where we were told to wear comfy clothes and Lucy, who I still had a bit of a crush on, turned up in leggings, to my

delight and despair and deathly agony. I spent the two hours looking *oh god anywhere else don't let her know*.

3. Pancake evening, Ellie making pancakes in the shapes of all our initials. Em had dyed her hair green in a fit of petulant indie-kid hope: it hadn't quite gone to plan, more swamp creature than manic pixie dream girl, but she laughed it off, and I thought it looked cool, desperately cool.

4. An evening where I brought my clarinet and Em her guitar and we played some Beatles songs together. She sang. Maybe Holly bought her guitar too. Kyle, I think, turned up with some assorted percussion instruments. How are some things so clear and others so vague? All I remember, really, is how that evening before Explorers started, Em played me Joan Baez's 'Diamonds and Rust' for the first time. Talk about foreshadowing. *Well, I'll be damned / here comes your ghost again.*

OBVIOUSLY, we were in love. I didn't know this for a while. Actually, as it turned out, Max told me.

One evening Em and I went for a walk to a different park: not the Garrison near me, but one towards town, excellent for dog walks. We'd been there recently when I decided to break up with a boy I was seeing, Colm, someone I'd met at Em's then-boyfriend's 18th birthday party. The two of us had spent the night in London but gotten lost – we went to an experimental concert put on by one of her relatives first, and then got the right bus but in the wrong direction, ending up in Canary Wharf rather than Mile End as intended – so we were late to the party. She spent a lot of the evening flirting with someone else, leaving me to flirt and chat to this sweet boy I ended up briefly seeing. Both relationships had long dissolved by this point, though – Colm and I because he had gone to university and I decided the distance wasn't worth it with everything else (every*one* else, maybe) going on; Em and Zaki for more or less the same reason, or because by that point she'd met someone else.

I tell this anecdote purely to illustrate how connected our

lives had become. We knew the same people, fancied the same people – you'd need a flow chart to explain it all – and spent so much of our time together that you'd have been forgiven for thinking there were no secrets between us at all. At times we forgot we were separate people. We knew each other. I knew without asking that she hated herself too.

Anyway, for whatever reason that night we decided to go back to the same park. It had been raining, and it was dark: Em was regretting the decision by the time we'd got there. She had a deep-rooted fear of slugs and we'd already seen several. I can't remember which one of us made the suggestion that there was a strange man watching us – maybe there even was, certainly we weren't the only two out for a walk – but it was an excuse to leave as much as anything, and then suddenly exhilarated she had grabbed my hand and we were *sprinting* towards the main road. Less of a run more of a flight, a spontaneity, a gasping for something that might have been more than oxygen High with it, laughing on the way back, I texted Max to tell him about my evening and he said – the words seared themselves into my brain in a way that I have never and will never forget – *you know you're in love with her, don't you?*

xxvii

HE *had* texted me, of course. And this time he hadn't disappeared after a week or so.

I sometimes wish he had. I shouldn't – what's the point of wishing? – and I would always have wondered. But... But there are always those things, aren't there, that you'd just like to *know* what would happen if you went back in time and changed it, whether or not it would have changed the whole course-spiral-inevitability of the way things unfolded. Wishes aside, I'm just curious. Would things have been better? Sometimes I think, maybe not, maybe I was doomed to everything that came afterwards either way. But more frequently I think, well, how could it not have been better? There is no doubt either way that things would have been *different* if he hadn't ever texted me again, if he'd disappeared from my world after the Jamboree and become just another story to tell. It would have broken my heart, yes. But there are worse things.

He texted me a couple of days after we'd come back, and although I was initially furious with him for not having come to say goodbye to me in Sweden, we soon fell into an easy pattern. *Easy* only in a certain respect. Like falling into a magnetic field. Like bleeding. Like breathing. I had wanted him for so long having him felt almost like happiness.

We texted all the time. I mean *all the time*, every day: in lessons taking quick glances at the phone hidden on my lap, muscle memory for the keys as I typed out my response; at night until one of us fell asleep. I texted him when I was with Em until she scorned me for being obsessed with my phone, for constantly needing it near me, which is still a terrible habit I have to this day, a hangover from the fear of not being in contact. For a while we ended every text message with two hearts: <3 <3. He called me *sweetheart* when he was happy. He called me *darling*.

He wasn't often happy.

He had a girlfriend called Sofia for a bit and told me about her one night when we ended up sexting anyway. When she broke up with him at Christmas he called me crying, sent me pleading text messages, and my aunt saw the phone screen and said *that's a lot of kisses!* assuming it was my boyfriend.

I went to London for a night to stay with my uncle and met Max in Waterloo Station. I was reading *Anna Karenina* and saw no irony in that fact. We wandered Oxford Street and found a Café Rouge for dinner: he had chicken caesar salad, I had a large glass of wine. He took me to my uncle's house, the two of us drunk and giggling on the tube, arguing about whether lizards have hands or feet, and he kissed me. I lay in a strange bed that night and cried.

Meanwhile, Em and I dipped in and out of various intertangled relationships. I lost my virginity to a guy who was best friends with the boy she was dating. One evening we all got drunk and stripped naked together ('strip Monopoly', the rules of which were immediately lost to a haze of vodka) and he tied me to my bed with my Scout neckers. Another time his friend and I were making out and Em and her boyfriend were hiding under my bed laughing. Another time, I was at my desk pretending to do Latin homework as the two of them kissed in my bed two metres away, my iPod playing a Pogues album on repeat. I dated a guy called Ollie and cheated on him with another guy called Ollie; they looked the same, they both treated me badly. I was in love with Max and with Em, with everyone. I cried myself to sleep almost every night I was alone, every night I wasn't falling asleep in my jeans with Em resting on me.

Max wanted to kill himself. His arms were littered with cuts; he wore a red bandana around his wrists to hide them. We had an established routine whenever he was sad and needed my attention. He would text me:

> *Heyy. How're you??*
> *Okay :)*
> *Hmmm. Only okay???*
> *I'm good! How're you?*

(I made this particular exchange up but in doing so the rhythms of how he spoke came back to me like a wave. I feel breathless: some memories are so fucking physical. Texting him like this was engrained in my body, if you cut it open you would still find it somewhere, the appendix maybe. The multiple question marks, the disbelieving whenever I said I was okay – or even good! – the way he always asked me how I was first, so that I would reply with the same question, so that he could open his sadness up to me and claim that I had asked.) If I didn't play the game, he would send dramatic declarations of self-harm and then stop answering for hours. *I can only speak to you* he told me *you are the only person who could save my life*.

If it was really bad, his sadness, then I would call him, though I hate speaking on the phone. Sometimes he would answer. When he did so it was my role to distract him, get him to breathe. We would either play the questions game, where I fired questions at him: *what is your favourite animal* and *what is your happiest memory* and *what are you watching at the moment* or I would get him to talk about his obsessions, encourage him to speak. He owned more horror films than anyone else I knew, kept hundreds of DVDs in boxes organised alphabetically; he loved Stephen King (in the first year we didn't speak I bought myself a charity shop copy of *Bag of Bones* and terrified myself reading it, persisting only in case it worked like a spell, in case somehow he knew what I was doing for him, embracing him into every little aspect of my life); he could talk for hours about whatever tv show he was into at that time, or about whatever he was learning on the piano. I would drop one of these topics into conversation hoping to distract him away from his sadness. But when he was unresponsive, unable even to glean enthusiasm for Kevin Bacon's role in *Friday the 13th* or to argue about why Gimli was the best character in the *Lord of the Rings,* I would talk instead. I would talk about the flat we would live in in London one day, him working in the West End and performing in the evenings, me spending my days writing. He wanted tamed panthers as pets; he wanted to get married in a dinosaur suit. We would watch Disney films and have threesomes with beautiful men and women, I told him, and he would laugh through his tears and say he loved me.

Sometimes he wouldn't answer. He would text me incoherently, drunkenly, panic stricken, telling me he was covered in his own blood, telling me only I could help, only I could save his life. And when I called him sobbing, the phone would ring out, and I'd leave answerphone messages begging, and eventually I'd fall asleep tear-stained, my phone next to me like a lifeline (silenced except for his number, so that if he called I could always answer), wrapped in the cables of the iPod headphones I'd be listening to songs too loudly on, desperately trying to stay awake. This is another reason so many of those late teenage nights were spent dressed, falling asleep in jeans or school clothes, wearing the same underwear for days, sneaking out leaving my friends draped over my sofas to sext Max or to beg him to survive. Or both.

Sometimes he wouldn't text me the next day, either, and I would get up and go to school or to work and spend the whole time thinking with a deathly sick certainty about how, when I went to check my phone, there would be a message from the police or the hospital or his mum telling me it had finally happened. Whenever it didn't – whenever I went into the break room at the zoo to check my phone having spent five hours nonstop serving ice cream or chips only to be confronted with *nothing* when I fully expected him to be dead – it was always a shock. I don't know how I lived like that for over a year, haunted by the ghost of a death that never came, permanently on the edge of grief. Afterwards, I would be furious, try to make him understand how *fucking worried I was don't you know how much I love you* and he would apologise and say he hated himself for it I deserved better and I would say *no, it's not your fault I'm sorry, I just care, I just want to be able to help you* or I would say *I can't do this anymore* and we wouldn't talk for a week until one of us broke. Until he texted me saying he needed me, or – more frequently – I texted him, driven to it by the fear that he might be dead and *I wouldn't know* and it would be, how could it not be, *my fault*. And because I loved him, despite or because of it all.

And when I did get through to him he would say I helped. He would say I had saved his life. And how can you resist that? Wouldn't denying it be akin to murder? If I didn't answer, and he wasn't lying – wouldn't I have killed the person I loved?

Once he played the piano for me down the phone and he said it was the last time he would ever play, that it was the only thing he'd miss, and I told him *then think about that, live for that,* collapsed on the floor of my bedroom trying not to scream about the fact that he wouldn't miss me –

I would have said anything to help him. *Live for me. Live for me. If there's nothing else, live because you love me.* I felt my own worth crumbling beneath me. What good was I if I couldn't do this, if I poured everything I had into one of the two people who meant the most to me in all the world and it meant nothing. What good was my love? What good my words?

We went shopping and bought each other books: *The Shining* for me, *The Wasp Factory* for him. He sent me a postcard from New York. I took the train to Sussex, once, and met his mum. I saw his house. He played me songs from

Bare: the musical, his current favourite:

> *Do you remember*
> *that day that you met me?*
> *I swear it was yesterday, I knew with a glance.*
> *That you were the question,*
> *and you were the answer.*
> *That the world would make sense again if I held your hand.*

We got takeaway Chinese and slept together on the sofa. When I asked him why he didn't have full penetrative sex with me that night, he said: *because I want it to be special when we do*. We were both sleeping with other people. There was a girl whose name he mentioned occasionally, but I was used to living with jealousy by now. I didn't ask questions, I didn't want to know.

xxviii.i

WHAT can you remember about the worst night of your life?

Everyone has one, or some. Deaths. Bad news. Break-ups. The night at university when I was raped should be mine with no competition. But in reality, when I think of nights that pound my head deep into my stomach, nights that sicken time and unravel all the things you are holding on to, it is the night of my eighteenth and all it came to represent that I think of first.

I was dating Ollie – the first Ollie – though our relationship, such as it was, was falling rapidly apart. He had gone to university and spent days forgetting to reply to me; despite it being his reading week, he had chosen not to come back for my birthday. I had cheated on him, or was going to cheat on him, in a sad, gin-fuelled drinking game with the second Ollie, who was a Jehovah's Witness who would not admit his attraction to me in public, who would spend several months pretending we were not together. Neither of them were coming to my birthday night out. But I didn't care. Max was. Em was.

Before Max came, I asked Em to be careful around him. I was in love with them both; more importantly, I knew them both well enough to suspect that attraction would flare between them. Em had already kissed people she'd known I liked, but that was different. *Of course* she said, she wouldn't do anything, she wouldn't do that to me. She was suspicious of him and all the hurt he'd caused me, she said, but she would aim to get on with him for my sake.

We ate at a local Vietnamese restaurant and came back to my house to pre-drink. I held Max's hand on the way back, whilst my friends pretended not to notice. I told him, *I'm so glad you came*.

We ran out of vodka and wine; my friend Freya and I went to the Sainsbury's round the corner to buy more. Already drunk, I confessed my anxiety to her, and she reassured me: they wouldn't do that. But when we got back, Em and Max were lying together on my bed, and Freya caught my eye. Max said "darling" and both Em and I replied: "yes." But nothing had happened, nothing, nothing.

We carried on drinking, the four of us lying together.

More friends arrived.

We were drunk.

We started walking into town.

The rest happens in quick flashes, a bad PowerPoint presentation:

1) as we're walking into town – *to celebrate my eighteenth*

birthday – Ollie calls me and breaks up with me.

2) I collapse, crying, crying.

3) We do shots. I beg Em not to kiss Max, I tell her I felt the energy between them, I tell her I love him, she says, *I know, I won't. I know.*

4) We go to the club, and we drink more, and I kiss Max breathless so in love, and we are in the smoking area and I kiss Em breathless so in love, I kiss them both that night and I dance and I dance and I trust them I love them.

5) I take my shoes off to walk home and I take Max to my bed.

6) In the morning Em and I walk him to the station together, and she watches me kiss him goodbye.

xxviii.ii

THE walk to the station was beautiful with Em. We did it so frequently: going to meet people, going to London together, picking each other up, keeping each other company. We would get coffees on the way and burn our hands or stain our clothes, because we always walked too fast and they always filled the mugs too full. If only one of us had to go there, usually, the other one would come too, make some excuse, anything for the walk, for the extra time together, for crossing the river and seeing the dappled Essex Tudor houses reflected in the water. So of course she came with me to say goodbye to Max: I didn't even question it. She stood back awkwardly as I kissed him.

Our own kissing last night was in the air, not heavy, just present. But we were both hungover and I had his come in my hair, I was wearing leggings without any underwear, I had the aftermath of being dumped to deal with. And it didn't matter, really, it didn't seem to change anything, I already knew by then that I loved her. So we didn't talk about it: I left her at her house and went back to mine to change into the teletubbies jumper she'd made for me, planning to lie on my bed and listen to some new CDs and have a nap. She had painted me an oil painting of the sea, a whale breaking through in a spray of purple and blue and green. I was lying on my bed looking at it when she texted me.

And then she told me:

> *I love you. I'm in love with you. I didn't think I was, but I am.*

And then she told me:

> *I kissed Max.*

xxviii.iii

EM *Em, Em*, I wrote in my diary that night, *I love you too, of course I love you.*

xxviii.iv

THE next day at school Freya said: *did Em tell you?*

She saw them kissing and said they had 24 hours to tell me, or she would. She was furious for me. But I barely cared about the betrayal. I went to school giddy with it: Em *loved* me; the kisses weren't mistakes; we were in love. We could be together, maybe. Whatever existed between us could maybe shift to the centre to be seen by everyone else. We could admit how much it mattered. I had already invited her to the Christmas ball at my school. Her friends would be going. But I thought she could come not as my friend but as my date, I pictured us standing together dressed in black tie, displaying our connection to the world, to all the boys we'd dated or flirted with or kissed in front of each other. A final statement: *this is what matters. We are each other's, were never yours.* We had both been hurt and heartbroken by those boys that past year, but we could go together to the ball and it would all be better. It would all cease to matter.

She came round and lay next to me on my bed as she had so many times before. We turned the lights off and listened to 'Cecilia'. She rested her hand on my knee, uncertain.

That week I was – buoyant. Max reconciled things with

the girl he sometimes mentioned and it didn't hurt me too much. I didn't care about his kissing Em. All my jealousy had crystallised into happiness. *I love you I'm in love with you* she had said. *I didn't think I was but I am.*

Then we started fighting. I can't explain why. Initially it was because she said she didn't want to go to the ball with me. If you're that close to someone, a tiny bit of distance is enough to make the whole thing unbearable. Our own closeness acted as a crowbar. The magnetic poles reversed. Her and her ex had sex and he lied about using a condom, and I despised her for it, not realising he had raped her. I was so wrapped up in my misery – Max's misery – that, this time, I ignored hers.

Then I went to visit a university and didn't check my phone for just one day, and that was when Max tried to kill himself.

xxviii.v

HE texted me from the ambulance. He had drunk a bottle of bleach. I always thought his death would come from the blood he was so fond of, but suddenly I was scrolling through sites about stomach pumping and poison, not letting myself sleep although he was unconscious by now or at least not replying, and I was choking on the guilt.

It's only writing this all these years later that I wonder if it was even true –

Em cut herself too. More and more I found myself obsessing over it. Could *that* be why they had kissed? Was it a bond they shared that let them understand each other in a way I never could? And what did it say about me, that the two people I lived for both hated themselves like that? What did it say about my love?

All at once everything collapsed. Em was pregnant and we couldn't talk without fighting and I was crying drunkenly down the phone to Max, sitting on a roundabout surrounded by traffic as New Year's Eve ticked over into a New Year, and he was telling me he would always love me, we were falling asleep on the phone together, and Em hadn't spoken to me in weeks, and my love was corroding into something evil and murderous, and then it was February and Em was getting an abortion and I wasn't there to hold her hand like I should have been, and I'd slept with my ex and then he'd dumped me *again*, and I had a litre bottle of vodka hidden under my bed, and I was learning what it meant to lose an evening in alcohol, and Em hadn't responded to my texts and I was excelling at school and my boyfriend was hurting me and I deserved it all.

I'm sorry I can't be more specific. But it all happened at once. I can't unpick it – the screaming rush of memories. I told no-one about any of it. To do so would have been to open my skin and reveal how deeply, deeply fucking evil I truly was. Nothing else could explain it: I loved him and he wanted to die. I loved her and she saw me in a way that no-one else could and rejected it. She hated herself and it felt like a mirror shining back on my own unworth. I knew that there was something fundamentally broken inside of me. That I twisted people away into loathing. That Max and Em had kissed each other, wound meeting wound, like it had been me who wielded the carefully unpicked razor blade.

xxviii.vi

1 May 2012. We were walking back from Scouts. It was a perfect spring evening – dark, touched with magic, something essential in the air.

We walked past a tree coming into blossom. Giant ballet-pink orbs suspended above our heads. And green leaves – 'leaves greener than they have right to be' – and finally, rising above it all, lighting everything up, a single street lamp. The effect was breathtaking, like stumbling across a painting that had been hidden for decades, like discovering a new colour, like seeing a crack in the universe and watching as something you never dared imagine seeps through it. We lay down on the pavement: she rested her head on my lap. No-one walked past. We lay there for maybe half an hour, just on the ground, just staring up: sharp green, creamy pink, brilliant electric light. Ink-black sky. We were afraid to leave. You can never get something like that back. I knew it as well as she did. Afterwards, I wrote a poem:

> 'Lying here on the dirty cold-grey ground,
> We both know that when we stand to go,
> We will never find this world again. And so
> We stay.'

6 February 2013. I thought we were meeting to reconcile. Instead, everything ended.

We met in our Costa, the one attached to a cinema. I was there first. Normally, I liked killing time there waiting for her. We could sit there for hours in a moving stream of people, the only constant. People loitering before their showing; people meeting their friends off the bus outside, *a quick stop before hitting the shops?*; people booking tickets and grabbing a drink at the same time; people who wanted a cappuccino with their popcorn; people caught in the rain on their way home from work deciding to wait it out with a hot chocolate. I liked the way that it wasn't a destination in itself for anyone except us.

One of the things you forget about break ups is how strange they are. The whole texture of the world shifts. Things mutate into stark reminders of memories you didn't know you had. So: suddenly a song becomes a knife wound, a punch to the stomach, a physical reminder, Heathcliff's 'the entire world is a dreadful collection of memoranda that she did exist, and that I have lost her' of all or any of the other clichés you turn to. A meal you ate together. The t-shirt she recommended. A book you discussed. et cetera and the rest forever.

She broke up with me next to the cinema, and left me crying amongst people who were only there waiting for something better to come along –

She said: *I've been trying to cut everything poisonous out of my life*. And I thought: *oh, good, we're talking like normal again.*

She continued: *but somehow you keep worming yourself back in*. And I realised I was the poison.

She said: *don't you have anything to say for yourself?* And I didn't – how could I? of course she was right. So I said nothing. I watched her walk away.

I broke.

HOW much more misery can you take? The depths of teenage angst, huh? I don't want to skirt over it, but I don't want to needlessly drag you down into the petty, small, world-destroying mess of being eighteen.

This is supposed to be a book about *camping*, isn't it? When did that stop?

I have told parts of this story over and over, but it never occurred to me until now that the true thrust of it wasn't ever about Max.

A *Financial Times* article about the Jamboree says: 'its conformity also means, despite all of Bear [Grylls'] magic, that in Britain at least, scouting still isn't particularly cool.' The same article also mentions that 'there are now half-a-million British scouts and 33,000 on the waiting list'. Coolness isn't everything, and I am not so plagued by this apparent discrepancy that I need to address it, but – I want to speak to those half-a-million. I want to say: you were not wrong, in those moments it felt like the version you which existed on camp was somehow more real. You were not wrong to think it was important.

Therapy is about stories. The worst thing about trauma

is the way it shatters your recollections. Those few months – Max's suicide attempt, Em breaking my heart – are fractured beyond recognition for me and possibly always will be. Slowly, though, you move away from the initial trauma, the way it is so *immediate* and *jarring*, and you form it into a narrative: ah, so this happened. Then this. Then this.

You tell yourself. Then you tell a friend. Maybe you tell a therapist. You float amongst memories and force them to form a jigsaw shape of narrative. If only you can do that, then you can start to heal...

That's a lie. The story telling *never ends*. It's not just about getting to a point where you have a tale to tell. It's about getting to a point where you're not interested in telling it. When you have other things to say. When you can leave it alone. Until then, you write and rewrite it, you tell and retell it, casting yourself as the antagonist, then the victim, then applying a level of nuance like glossy paint, then tearing it all apart, renouncing narrative, then coming back, seeing what happens when you add another character in –

So, you understand that although Thriftwood ceased to throb between Max and I, the beginning and end of the story still resonates from there. Time passed, somehow. Scouts stretched into the past. Em stopped coming: I won that, I suppose, a hollow victory in her abandonment. We all went to separate universities, and although I meant to come back in the holidays, volunteer as a leader along with Holly and Ellie, it never quite worked out like that, I never quite managed to stay in touch.

Here is what happened next: that girl, the one who Max told me about, the one he was with when I turned eighteen and we slept in my bed, Em's kisses on both our lips, was fourteen.

Here is what happened next: he raped her.

Here is what happened, and I hope by now it is clear that I still believe this despite it all: he loved me. Somehow, in some way. He loved me even if it wasn't good. He would have trusted me, he would have told me about her, if I'd asked. I could have – I could have known, at least. I could have done something.

I believed that I saved his life and that meant that what he did to her was my responsibility too. If I had not saved him, she would have been saved.

Here is what happened next: when I was raped by one of my best friends in Cambridge, it was Max who came on Skype and watched *Frozen* with me. It was Max who I called up whenever drunk that year, lost in the same sickly cycle of self-harm that had plagued both of them. (If they understood each other because of it, could I not make amends the same way?) It was Max who could leave me thirty missed calls one night threatening suicide and still ask me how I was the next morning like things were equal between us; Max, who asked me to play our old game of distraction whenever one or both of us was spiralling down.

I'm worried that after the two of them, there isn't enough of you left to love me, said my boyfriend. *I'm worried you would choose Max over me, if he asked you to. I'm worried you would never cry like that over me.*

It was Max who comforted me when I cried for hours in the snow after Em walked away.

It was Max I texted drunk at a party *darling I adore you,* causing my friend-rapist to snatch my phone out of my hand and say *you should be with me* as he pinned me against the wall in fury –

Eventually, after three years of arguments and wine and blood and the way we came crawling back to each other again and again, I came to take my final university exams. Of course they started the same week that Max's rape trial started. By then he had dropped out of his music course, or maybe been forced out. For three hours a day I sat in a room with my own rapist writing on tragedy and Renaissance plays, before going back to my room and refreshing the live feed of Max's trial, obsessively. I started smoking again. Everyone said: *how are you dealing with the exams?* and I couldn't begin to explain: *what's Hecuba to him, or he to Hecuba..*

Max texted me after every day in court, need seeping out

of his words. I hated him. I hated him. I told myself I wouldn't reply, then did, choked by the thought of his death.

He was found not guilty due to lack of evidence. I have no doubt that he did it. I never did. He may have thought he loved her, but he has never understood the way that love falls separate from possession. After all, we had owned each other.

Secretary of the Gender and Feminism society, an outspoken feminist, I kept my twisted inability to say no to him secret. He continued to call me drunk with need and grief. He still held his life like a threat over mine. And I had already failed his victim by being too jealous to ask her name; I couldn't bring myself to fail him too.

I still believe that, somewhere inside me. But I am trying to live by something I read in Lucia Osborne-Crowley's book on trauma: 'I must release myself from the spectre of the victims I didn't protect.' I must absolve myself of the weight of her name. Of all of it.

THAT*he turns up all swagger and bad shirts and the secret is, the secret you are only just beginning to understand is, that just because you like someone doesn't not mean they are not cruel, it does not excuse them.* I am so disgusted with myself *you* think I am such a hypocrite *because here you are it's a cold September afternoon and you're on the Southbank starting your new life New You in London and the very first thing of any importance you've done, dinner last night and setting up the TV and breakfast this morning after uncomfortable first night in a too-big-bed strained-sleep don't count, the first thing you've done and will remember doing is this coffee-blustery walk with him. Him who you haven't seen for a lifetime, a whole town and sub-heading of your life has passed without him intruding (physically) and when he says at the* end I haven't seen you for it must be two years *and you say* four *your voice is like ice it's a weapon, it's a betrayal that he hasn't been counting the months. He is taken aback, like he never had anyone in his life for that long before which is probably true but nonetheless. And even though you didn't talk for at least one of those years, back-to-back long days where you thought* I don't need him *and felt buoyed up by it now here you are with all that pride like a belt beating you down, it's still four years, the inescapable sickness of which is the realisation that maybe* *you are right in those treacle late thoughts in the dark. You will never escape him. Here is all the proof you need, that life stretches back and it is you limply hanging on to a friendship unimportant enough for him that two and four years blur into one whilst you carry the scars of every conversation you've ever had, you could probably recite them all. He hugs you goodbye and you think why aren't I crying and maybe that's the real bitterness of it all, that you are betraying your morals and the foundations of your beliefs for someone you can't even cry over anymore or maybe there are just no tears left they've disappeared like everything else you ever had of him. You gave his shorts to your brother and you burnt his card and you forced yourself not to blush whenever ordered a caramel latte with an extra shot of espresso and yet here you are with nothing to say, sitting on the Southbank dressed like an adult facing the person you hate and love and feel nothing for and always will, a prison-sentence always for life, a fitting punishment for your crime.*

xxxi

I will never speak to Max again. But I search his name on the internet, sometimes, to find out whether he is still alive. I keep his number on WhatsApp so I can see that he was last active and I don't have to choke with the fear that he has died and I will never know.

I went to therapy and I stopped hurting myself. I don't know if the impulse ever goes away, once you know you *can*. But I no longer want to. I think of the girl whose pain I fitted into mine, and I am sorry. I think of the people I hurt in my own howl, the destruction misery can cause, and I am sorry. I offer myself sympathy: I was fifteen, and he gave me the responsibility of his life. That would fuck anyone up.

I tried, at first, to tell myself that I never loved Max, which was a lie so huge I couldn't build anything on it. Instead I have reconciled myself to the truth: I loved him. I believe he loved me. And I am not failing that fact by moving on.

Here are the scenes I want to end on:

Ellie and I in a tent. Holly and her boyfriend Scott in the campervan. "Budge over", Ellie says, and she has a girlfriend, and I have a boyfriend, and the two of us have somehow fallen into something more like adulthood. We've somehow made it through. We all live in different cities, and we keep in touch;

we all love each other. Here we are in Chester, celebrating Holly's 21st birthday.

& here are Ellie and I as her bridesmaids. Tony, Chris, Laura, Fleur at the wedding. I am full of love, good love, healthy love.

& Em reaching out to me; the most unbelievable message, after three years of missing her. The first time we meet as adults. A picnic in the park. Finding a place in each other's lives with forgiveness: not the all-or-nothing we promised each other, once, but something realistic, something I am grateful for, a friendship. I send her the first draft of this book and she tells me she would read more. She tells me she remembers it all too. *Here comes your ghost again.* I think of us at seventeen living with our souls so close that ultimately we couldn't help but hurt each other, and I am glad to know her.

& how I told this story for so many years, but I was wrong. I've worn these tracks of memory again and again, and it's only all these years later I realized how deeply I missed the point at the time. All those people I would never have met otherwise. All those people I would never have learnt to love.

& I talk to my friends in the midst of a pandemic and I say 'I'm writing a book about Scouts' and the memories and recollections and joy floods in from people I see all the time and people I haven't seen in years. This is the Scouts I want to remember; this is the story I want to tell. *On my honour, I promise.*

Works cited

A Midsummer Night's Dream, dir. by Nicholas Hytner (The Bridge Theatre, 3ʳᵈ June - 31 August 2019)

Baden-Powell, Robert, *Scouting for Boys: A Handbook for Instruction in Good Citizenship,* ed. by Elleke Boehmer (Oxford: Oxford University Press, 2005)

Brontë, Emily, *Wuthering Heights* (1845) (London: Penguin Books, 2003)

Buffy the Vampire Slayer, 'Seeing Red', UPN, 7 May 2002

Carr, J. L., *A Month in the Country* (1980) (London: Penguin Books, 2000)

Carson, Anne, *Autobiography of Red* (London: Jonathan Cape, 1999)
-- *The Glass Essay*, in *Glass and God* (London: Jonathan Cape, 1998)

De Abaitua, Matthew, *The Art of Camping* (London: Penguin Books, 2012)

Larkin, Philip, 'Home is so sad' (1958) in *Collected Poems* (London: Faber & Faber, 2003)

London, Jack, *The Call of the Wild* (1903) (London: Puffin Books, 1994)

Millard, Rosie, 'Hold on to your woggles', *Financial Times* (19 August 2011)

Osborne-Crowley, Lucia, *I Choose Elena* (London: The Indigo Press, 2019)

Peep Show, 'Quantocking', Channel 4, 16 Dec 2005

Riddel, Chris, *The Edge Chronicles: Beyond the Deepwoods* (London: Random House, 2006)

Rowling, J. K., *Harry Potter and the Deathly Hallows* (London: Bloomsbury, 2007)
–– *Harry Potter and the Goblet of Fire* (London: Bloomsbury, 2000)

Shakespeare, *A Midsummer Night's Dream* (1595), in *The Oxford Shakespeare,* ed. by John Jowett, William Montgomery, Gary Taylor and Stanley Wells, 2nd edn (Oxford: Oxford University Press, 2005)
–– *Hamlet* (1599-1601), in *The Oxford Shakespeare,* ed. by John Jowett, William Montgomery, Gary Taylor and Stanley Wells, 2nd edn (Oxford: Oxford University Press, 2005)

Stewart, Nikita, 'Inside the Creation of a Girl Scout Troop Unlike Any Other', *Literary Hub Online* (24 June 2020)

Thoreau, Henry David, *Walden; or, Life in the Woods* (1854) (London: Vintage, 2017)

Waugh, Evelyn, *Brideshead Revisited* (1945) (London: Penguin Books, 2000)

SONGS

ABBA – 'Super Trouper'

The Beautiful South – 'A Little Time'

The Carpenters – 'Top of the World'

The Carpenters – 'Yesterday Once More'

Cast Recording – 'Bare', from *Bare: A Pop Opera*

Europe – 'The Final Countdown'

Joan Baez – 'Diamonds and Rust'

Simon and Garfunkel – 'Cecilia'

Miley Cyrus – 'Party in the USA'

Taylor Swift – 'Love Story'

The Vaccines – 'A Lack of Understanding'

Yuck – 'Suck'

Acknowledgements

THANK you to everyone who talked to me about our shared pasts, who let me tell their stories, who has been there throughout it all. Thank you especially to 'Ellie's A-team', the best friends I could ask for; to James for always being forgiving and a better person than I was, and for allowing me to dig up the past; to Ben, for reading this draft, for always asking if I was okay, and for many walks in Castle Park; to Chris, for all the music and for forgiving me for stealing your girlfriend and then breaking your heart; to Caz, Warwick, Jack, Kyle, and the rest of the Super Troupers; to Tony Jay, Chris Jay, Jenny Jay, Julie Jay, for everything you did (I'm sorry I was such a nightmare); and to Em, for saying exactly what I needed to hear, for being my first reader and my best reader, and for being my friend. Thank you to the counselling team at Solace Women's Aid who allowed me the space to talk. And thank you, always, to Laith. I promise never to make you sleep in a tent.

LAY OUT YOUR UNREST

www.ingramcontent.com/pod-product-compliance
Lightning Source LLC
Chambersburg PA
CBHW062100080426
42734CB00012B/2700